"A unique and different approach [...] I have read. So insightful, thoroughly scriptural, and profoundly balanced [...] the delicate handling of how spiritual warfare impacts our lives in relationships. Best of all, it is practical! This book will make a difference for you and your spouse as you discuss and act on Tim's very helpful suggestions and directives."

Roger Hershey, Cru speaker, ministry consultant, author of *The Finishers*

"As intimidating as the topic of spiritual warfare in marriage may seem to be, Muehlhoff's approach is an unthreatening treatment of this long-neglected but significant issue. No matter the current condition of their marriages—whether thriving, tedious, or troubled—Christians will benefit from reading this book."

Douglas S. Huffman, professor and associate dean of biblical and theological studies at Talbot School of Theology, Biola University

"This is a desperately needed book on an overlooked topic. *Defending Your Marriage* is a sobering reminder of an invisible but very real danger to every Christian marriage—spiritual attack. When we fail to protect ourselves from this threat, we leave the back door open to forces that can erode our love, weaken our commitment, and even destroy our marriage. Thanks to Dr. Muehlhoff for identifying our hidden enemy and giving us plans for a strong defense, and for doing it in such a readable and engaging style."

Tim Downs and **Joy Downs,** authors of *Fight Fair!*

"Once a couple refuses to settle for a fifth-rate relationship and decides to pursue a Christ-centered marriage, to learn how to look and live and love like our Lord, the attacks of the Adversary can feel overwhelming. Tim has given us a unique, biblically based, relevant handbook for not just protecting our marriage but in the process actually deepening and strengthening our love relationship with God and with each other. This practical and long-overdue resource will help you become 'more than conquerors' and experience the quality of marriage that God has designed for those who love him. It's a book you'll read more than once."

Gary J. Oliver, executive director of the Center for Healthy Relationships, professor of psychology and practical theology at John Brown University

"I have known Tim for thirty-six years, and I'm privileged to call him my friend. As a pastor, there's no one I would trust more on the issues addressed in this book. *Defending Your Marriage* is an excellent book, written by an even better man."

William Radford, senior pastor at Bedford Presbyterian Church, Bedford, Nova Scotia

"I am so grateful that Dr. Muehlhoff has taken on this critically important topic. *Defending Your Marriage* provides deep truths, engaging personal examples, and helpful insights into an area that too few authors have the authority to tackle. This book will set a standard for others that follow on this topic, providing couples with amazing resources to help them defend their marriage."

Chris Grace and **Alisa Grace,** founders of the Center for Marriage and Relationships at Biola University

"This is a must-read for Christian marital therapists! It fills an important gap in our training by providing practical tools for the therapist to acknowledge, identify, and respond to spiritual warfare in marriages. As a marital therapist I am often searching for ways to help couples that seem to not respond to traditional marital interventions. This book offers a new intervention: addressing spiritual warfare to help with the healing process for couples. I am excited that I now have a detailed map on how to address spiritual warfare in marriage beyond just naming it."

Jana Anderson, certified Gottman method couples therapist

"My wife, Karen, and I have long thought Tim has a unique gift for presenting God's word on marriage in a fresh and engaging way. May his teaching on this critical but rarely tackled subject reach and bless many."

Jeffery Justice, board certified surgeon

"*Defending Your Marriage* offers a much-needed examination of an often overlooked influence in marriage: spiritual oppression. Tim Muehlhoff reminds us of the importance of taking marriage and spirituality seriously, inviting each of us to look beyond ourselves, to the wisdom and insight of Scripture. This book serves as a resource to couples and communities alike, a call to intentionally serve God, one another, and our neighbors. An invitation to engage reality, believing in the power of God, prayer, and community, becoming beacons of hope and light in the process."

Robert Fisher, executive director, Center for Individual and Family Therapy

"*Defending Your Marriage* exposes Satan's tactics as it draws us to the Lord to experience his love, forgiveness, and power. As we extend the same to our spouses, we fortify our marriages. We imagine the impact this has not only on the health of our own marital relationship, but also on our communities as others enjoy the benefits of God's kingdom on earth being lived out in a family. We are looking forward to getting some friends together to discuss and practice the concepts in this book!"

Chris Zaugg and Susan Zaugg, former United States director of Digital Strategies for Cru

DEFENDING YOUR MARRIAGE

THE REALITY OF
SPIRITUAL BATTLE

TIM MUEHLHOFF

IVP Books

An imprint of InterVarsity Press
Downers Grove, Illinois

InterVarsity Press
P.O. Box 1400, Downers Grove, IL 60515-1426
ivpress.com
email@ivpress.com

InterVarsity Press® is the book-publishing division of InterVarsity Christian Fellowship/USA®, a
movement of students and faculty active on campus at hundreds of universities, colleges, and schools of
nursing in the United States of America, and a member movement of the International Fellowship of
Evangelical Students. For information about local and regional activities, visit intervarsity.org.

While any stories in this book are true, some names and identifying information may have been changed
to protect the privacy of individuals.

Cover design: David Fassett
Interior design: Jeanna Wiggins
Images: cicular flame: © Yamada Taro / Getty Images
        blue texture paper: © belterz / E+ / Getty Images
        wild herbs and spices: © ElenaMedvedeva / iStock / Getty Images Plus

ISBN 978-0-8308-4550-7 (print)
ISBN 978-0-8308-7382-1 (digital)

Printed in the United States of America ♾

InterVarsity Press is committed to ecological stewardship and to the conservation of natural resources in
all our operations. This book was printed using sustainably sourced paper.

Library of Congress Cataloging-in-Publication Data
Names: Muehlhoff, Tim, 1961- author.
Title: Defending your marriage : the reality of spiritual battle / Tim
   Muehlhoff.
Description: Downers Grove : InterVarsity Press, 2018. | Includes
   bibliographical references.
Identifiers: LCCN 2018028234 (print) | LCCN 2018030116 (ebook) | ISBN
   9780830873821 (eBook) | ISBN 9780830845507 (pbk. : alk. paper)
Subjects: LCSH: Marriage--Religious aspects--Christianity. | Spiritual
   warfare.
Classification: LCC BV835 (ebook) | LCC BV835 .M835 2018 (print) | DDC
   248.8/44--dc23
LC record available at https://lccn.loc.gov/2018028234

| P | 21 | 20 | 19 | 18 | 17 | 16 | 15 | 14 | 13 | 12 | 11 | 10 | 9 | 8 | 7 | 6 | 5 | 4 | 3 | 2 |
| Y | 35 | 34 | 33 | 32 | 31 | 30 | 29 | 28 | 27 | 26 | 25 | 24 | 23 | 22 | 21 | 20 | 19 | | | |

To Noreen, Michael, Jason, and Jeremy.

There is no one else I'd rather be in battle with than you!

CONTENTS

FOREWORD

CLINTON E. ARNOLD

The most extensive passage in Scripture about marriage (Eph 5) comes right before the most extensive passage about spiritual warfare (Eph 6). Is this coincidental? Not hardly.

In God's design, a good marriage depicts the love and intimacy that characterizes the relationship between Christ and his people, the church. And although Jesus assures us that the gates of hell will not prevail against the church, Satan relentlessly tries to take it down. So too with marriage.

As Tim Muehlhoff says in his introduction, "your marriage is a target." It's targeted because it represents a taste of heaven—God in close connection with his people. Satan wants to disrupt and oppose anything that attracts people to the loving and caring community he is working to establish on earth. By undermining marriages and driving spouses apart, Satan effectively destroys hope in the transcendent relationship to which marriages point.

For many people, whether they will openly admit it or not, speaking of demonic spirits and spiritual warfare is tantamount to living on the lunatic fringe of Christianity. Yes, this stuff is in the Bible, they admit, but it's better left in Bible times. If a couple is having difficulty in their marriage, they need the wisdom and help that comes from a seasoned marriage counselor, not some kind of demonic deliverance ritual. In fact, some worry that bringing demons into the picture could actually shift the focus away from what a couple may really need to work on to achieve a healthy marriage. But if the Bible is right on this issue, and the demonic realm really is interested in harming marriages, how can we afford to neglect it?

Imagine for a moment that I go to the doctor with a horrible sore throat that is a result of a bacterial infection. The doctor prescribes getting rest, gargling warm water with salt, and taking ibuprofen every six hours. By following this regimen, I will undoubtedly feel some measure of relief, but the doctor has not treated the root problem. I need antibiotics to fight the infection.

If your marriage is stuck in a loop of increasingly unhealthy interactions, have you stopped to consider that you may not be dealing with the root problem? There may be spiritual dynamics at work that require spiritual intervention.

This is where Tim's book comes in. The wisdom imparted in this volume will help you discern what is going on in your marriage and give you important tools for handling a wide array of issues that have spiritual roots.

In our culture, we've been socialized and educated to disregard the spiritual and think of the demonic as fantasy. But this isn't the biblical perspective. It's not the counsel of Jesus, Paul, or the apostles. They took this realm seriously and sought to integrate a spiritual warfare worldview into every aspect of daily life. Tim shows how this perspective is relevant to your marriage.

Introduction

WHEN YOUR MARRIAGE IS A TARGET

"He has a fever."

Unbelievable, I thought to myself as I listened to my wife's phone message. Last night our middle son felt a little warm, and we hoped it was nothing. No such luck.

"Could you swing by the pharmacy on your *way home?*"

You could hear the frustration in her voice. Her irritation was spurred on not only by an unexpected health issue but the fact that I was *still* at the office even though we had yet to pack. In the morning, my wife and I were flying out to speak at a marriage conference. It was an early flight and everything that could go wrong was happening—sick child, last-minute cancellation of a trusted sitter, and a yet-to-be completed deadline at work. The phrase, *everything but the kitchen sink* didn't seem so funny when we discovered later that night that our kitchen faucet was leaking *again*. The tension between us was high as we rode to the airport in silence.

After settling into our hotel room, we headed to the ballroom where the marriage conference was to be held to do a microphone check. We noticed conference volunteers walking up and down the rows pausing at each empty chair.

"What are they doing?" I asked the conference coordinator.

"Praying against spiritual forces," he responded.

His answer took me by surprise. After years of organizing Christian marriage conferences, the organizer took seriously the reality of spiritual opposition. He explained that the couples who would occupy these chairs have certainly faced many obstacles—sickness, travel delays, luggage lost in transit, unexpected financial pressures, and marital tension are all par for the course.

"Do we really think it's all coincidental?" he said laughing.

"Satan will do anything to keep us from working on our marriages. After all, a Christian marriage should reflect God's love. We'd be naive to think Satan isn't targeting us."

Walking back to our hotel room I was flooded with thoughts. *Is it really possible that Satan is targeting people attending this conference? Could it be that lost luggage or marital disagreements are not as innocent as they seem? And, if Satan is targeting people attending a conference, then certainly he'd attack people speaking at the conference. Right? Was my son's fever, a leaking kitchen pipe, and the tension between my wife and me Satan's attempt to discourage us? How can I tell if it's just a leaky pipe or something more threatening? Doesn't Satan have better things to do than target my wife and me?*

I was determined to get answers.

It is in contemplating these troubling ideas that *Defending Your Marriage* explores three specific questions. First, *why didn't I connect the dots the way the conference organizer did concerning spiritual battle?* To be honest, spiritual battle is simply not on my radar. Am I, a professor with a PhD, embarrassed by the possibility of spiritual oppression? As a modern follower of Christ, might this embarrass you as well? I wonder what Jesus or the apostle Paul would think about our skepticism. Second, *what is the purpose of a Christian marriage?* If, as Paul suggests in his letter to believers in Ephesus, Christian marriages are to be living metaphors of God's self-sacrificial love (Eph 5), then is it not prudent to expect and prepare for spiritual battle (Eph 6)? Third, *if we do acknowledge spiritual opposition, how can we be balanced?* How can we tell if an argument is just a difference of opinion between spouses or something else? And, if the something else turns out to be demonically influenced, how will we know and what can we do about it?

Thinking biblically entails seeing the world through the eyes of Scripture. Most Christians attempt to order their daily lives to fit the perspectives offered by biblical writers. We acknowledge that God exists, so we pray. We accept that death is not the final act, so we live in light of eternity. We know that God's love is for all, so we seek ways to share Christ's message with others. We embrace the Scriptures as God's communication to us, so we read it regularly. Yet what about the reality of Satan? "On this topic," suggests New Testament scholar Clint Arnold, "some of us suffer a double-mindedness. Although mental assent is given to the likelihood that evil spirits exist since it is affirmed in the Bible, in reality it makes no practical difference in the way we live our day-to-day lives."[1]

What would our marriages look like if we regularly sought productive ways to approach conflict, reclaimed our hectic schedules, carved out date nights, managed our finances better, sought to instill biblical values in our children, be Christian witnesses to our neighbors, *and* embraced the reality that we do all of these things while living in a spiritual war zone? "The Bible teaches not only that evil spirits exist, but also that they are actively hostile to all Christians; their perverse instigations adversely affect our day-to-day life and the lives of those around us," concludes Arnold.[2]

HOW WILL THIS BOOK HELP?

Defending Your Marriage approaches the topic of spiritual oppression in a balanced and biblical manner. The following features make the book useful and easy to apply:

1. Each chapter introduces readers to what Jesus and biblical authors have to say about Satan and spiritual forces at play today. Jesus did not merely talk abstractly about the reality of the devil; Satan personally tempted him for forty days in a wilderness outside of Jerusalem.

2. *Defending Your Marriage* helps readers understand why their marriages may invite spiritual opposition. By understanding God's design for marriage, readers will gain a better understanding of what Satan is so upset about and would want to target.

3. Couples are introduced to practical criteria that can be used to detect if spiritual oppression is at play. What are the most common indicators that Satan may be trying to derail your marriage?

4. *Defending Your Marriage* isn't merely a book about Satan. Rather, it's about how to protect our marriages by utilizing biblical tools such as prayer, meditating on God's Word, and mobilizing fellow believers.

5. Interspersed throughout the book are short interviews with Christian thinkers who have walked deeply with God. One of the great blessings of teaching at a Christian university is rubbing shoulders with individuals from diverse fields of study who can offer keen insight into spiritual battle.

FINDING THE RIGHT BALANCE

In reflecting on his own writings, C. S. Lewis often commented that his exploration of how demons interact with common people was his most important work. As he studied this neglected topic, he became convinced that many of us fall into two errors when it comes to the devil. One obvious error is to disbelieve the existence of Satan and demons altogether. The Bible simply speaks too much of their existence to ignore them. To take the Bible seriously entails opening ourselves to the reality of spiritual opposition to all aspects of our pursuit of Christ—including our marriages. However, an equally erroneous attitude is to "feel an excessive and unhealthy interest" in the demonic realm.[3] Lewis wryly concludes that the devil and his minions are equally pleased by both reactions.

As followers of Christ who seek to have thriving marriages, we must resist attributing every marital disagreement to demonic inducement, and likewise resist neglecting a spiritual reality embraced by Jesus and New Testament writers. After all, the reason we focus on the "schemes" of the devil (2 Cor 2:11) is to better understand how they could disrupt our strategies for cultivating a God-honoring marriage. By remembering and counteracting this forgotten threat, we not only pave the way for intimacy with our spouse, but also draw closer to our ultimate protector—God himself.

1

THE FIRST STEP

MAKING SENSE OF OUR ADVERSARY

I love my husband, but I just can't shake these thoughts."

Sandy sat before me holding her husband's hand, avoiding eye contact. She explained that after fifteen years of marriage and raising two kids she decided to get serious about her faith. They started going to church together and even doing occasional family devotions.

"Then out of the blue, I start having these crazy thoughts that perhaps we shouldn't have gotten married."

She squeezed her husband's hand knowing the pain such words caused. Over time, she was consumed by the realization that she didn't consult God when her husband proposed.

"What if God had someone else for me? What if he had an entirely different plan for my life? I can't stop asking all the *what ifs* . . . it's like a never-ending loop in my brain."

We went through the normal checklist: meeting with their pastor, marital counseling, praying for God's peace, memorizing

Scripture, and so on. She affirmed that they'd done all of that, and yet the thoughts kept coming.

"Am I crazy?" she said looking up.

"No," I responded. "I think you are under spiritual attack."

To my recollection, that was the first time I had ever suggested such a possibility. After thirty years of counseling couples and speaking at marriage conferences, it would not be my last. All couples experience the normal ups and downs of marriage: we argue and make up; we appreciate the strengths of our spouse even when those very strengths sometimes greatly annoy us; we struggle to forgive, but eventually do. Yet, after listening to couples—and my own experience—there are times when something else is going on. Times in a marriage when negative thoughts or anger simply will not go away. Like the woman at the beginning of the chapter, we get stuck in a continuous loop.

If that's your experience, what is the next step?

New Testament writers advocate that the *first step* isn't to learn a set of spiritual warfare techniques but, rather, to gather information. The apostle Paul writes to young believers in Corinth that in order to keep Satan from outwitting us we must become aware "of his schemes" (2 Cor 2:11). Early church leaders understood that following Jesus necessarily meant paying attention to the demonic. Christian author Kenneth Boa notes that "about 25 percent of Jesus' ministry as recorded in the Gospels involved deliverance from demonic affliction." He then draws a chilling conclusion, "The forces of evil did not disappear when Jesus left the earth."[1] If Jesus devoted so much time to the demonic realm and it still exists today, then why are significant segments of the modern church so reluctant to address it?

Far from learning about our opposition, many within the Western church simply ignore the reality of Satan. This aversion to spiritual opposition is not shared by our brothers and sisters within the global community. While spending a summer in Nairobi, Kenya, doing relief work with local churches, I was struck by how local leaders prayed for us. Before we'd head out, a leader would pray for God's protection against evil forces bent on disrupting our efforts.[2] Why are so many within the Western church leery to do the same?

IGNORING SATAN

Today, many are hesitant to focus on Satan for several reasons. First, one of the most persistent—and frustrating—stereotypes of Western Christians is that we are anti-intellectual. The fear of many Christians today is that taking Satan seriously will only add to the caricature that we put our brains on hold to embrace the demonic. Consider the following observations of some liberal religious writers. "It is impossible to use electric lights and the wireless and to avail ourselves of modern medical and surgical discoveries and at the same time believe in the New Testament world of spirits and miracles."[3] A belief in a literal Satan and demons is "outdated" and "throws away all credibility of theology."[4] "If we believe in demons then we might as well hold to a flat earth."[5] Those of us in academia are particularly sensitive to this reservation. What will non-Christian professors and scholars think when they learn I am taking seriously the topic of spiritual warfare? I can already imagine the snide comments and uncomfortable conversations. Similarly, what reactions would you get from neighbors or coworkers if you informed them of your acknowledgment of Satan?

Second, in our desire to be relevant we shy away from proclaiming a belief in demons. When I casually mentioned to a Christian friend that I was writing a book on spiritual battle to be shared at marriage conferences, a concerned look came across his face. "I thought our goal was to get people to Christian conferences, not drive them away. Bringing Satan into the mix is going to make people uncomfortable. Not sure it's a good idea." In the end, when our desire is to make conferences or churches "seeker friendly," we withhold vital biblical information that could significantly protect people.

Third, in a culture where individuals regularly avoid taking responsibility, we resist the urge to fall into the "devil made me do it" mentality. If we open the possibility that spiritual forces are inflaming my marital struggles, am I giving my spouse a perpetual out? "Sorry, Honey, my angry outburst was Satan getting the best of me! It's not entirely my fault!" Better we accept full responsibility for our own actions than give each other a demonic get-out-of-jail-free card. This attitude was reflected by a conferee at a marriage conference where I merely suggested Satan's *possible* involvement in marital struggles. He wrote in his evaluation, "I believe *too* much emphasis was placed on the power of Satan! He can't be everywhere!"

If we are honest, the main reason many of us shun embracing the possibility of the demonic is embarrassment. When we think of demonic influence we envision spinning heads, levitation, guttural voices speaking in Latin, religious fanatics performing exorcisms, and we feel foolish giving credence to *any* of it. But can we continue to ignore this issue?

Having watched the horrors of Nazi domination in Europe during World War II, German theologian Helmut Thielicke felt compelled to preach multiple sermons about spiritual battle. "Year by year we have seen an increasingly poisonous atmosphere settling down upon our globe and we sense how real and almost tangible are the evil spirits in the air" he began his famous series. "The overwhelming power of these experiences is so strong that it simply breaks through all the intellectual insulation which we are so prone to interpose in order to keep out these dark powers."[6]

While it would be erroneous to compare the current state of our world to the aftereffects of the second Great War, do you also have the feeling that an increasingly *poisonous atmosphere* is present today? As we watch the news, are we growing more and more concerned that our world, neighbors, and loved ones are a type of target, and that the challenges we face are not all tied to human interactions? As we watch another marriage end or family be blown apart, are we finally willing to admit that *something else* is going on? Following Thielicke's example, perhaps it's time to break through our cultural and intellectual insulation. What would it look like to take the issue of spiritual battle as seriously as Jesus and the Scriptures? To begin, let us consider a view of Satan informed by the Scriptures rather than pop culture.

 How Satan has been portrayed throughout the centuries has taken an interesting turn. Early images of Satan from the 1500s projected him as a bestial character complete with horns and hooves. Slowly, Satan started to take on human qualities, as in a 1978 painting *The Devil as Tailor*, where he is pictured as an ordinary man sewing German SS uniforms during World War II. In the 2015

television show *Lucifer,* he receives a complete makeover as a well-dressed, handsome, LA businessman with a surprising soft spot for helping others. Has the transition from horned beast to compassionate entrepreneur contributed to a gradual lowering of our defenses toward this demonic threat?

A BIBLICAL VIEW OF SATAN

The reason we take spiritual warfare seriously is not because we've had personal experiences with demons, known friends who have hair-raising stories, or seen YouTube videos of seemingly credible exorcisms. "The primary witness to the reality and existence of Satan is not experience or sensational stories," notes theologian Paul Enns, "but the testimony of Scripture."[7] Embracing the Bible as a God-inspired book that helps us view the world as *it really is* necessarily entails a robust belief in the spiritual realm. This includes believing not only that evil exists, but is personified in the person of Satan. Every New Testament writer makes reference to Satan, and Jesus specifically mentions him twenty-five times.[8] Yet who is this mysterious figure?

The name Satan comes from a Hebrew word that means *adversary.*[9] Thus Satan fundamentally opposes God and his plans. But how did an angelic being described as "full of wisdom and perfect in beauty" (Ezek 28:12) come to be God's adversary? What led to such rebellion? Two Old Testament authors give us a glimpse into what put Satan on such a traitorous trajectory.

Old Testament prophets Ezekiel and Isaiah both give us key information about this cosmic rebellion by first critiquing a human leader gone bad and then moving on to Satan himself.[10] In commenting on the ruler of Tyre, Ezekiel condemns him for gross human pride in proclaiming that he is powerful, wealthy, and skilled, leading to the final self-assessment that he is "a god" (Ezek 28:2). What could prompt a man to be so arrogant? Ezekiel gives us an answer by shifting his focus from the ruler of Tyre to the true king of Tyre, who inflamed this human leader's pride, Satan. The prophet then moves away from considering a human king and describes an angelic power. The qualities used to describe this cosmic influence could not possibly be true of any mortal leader. We learn that this being was, in the beginning, anointed as a cherub (prominent angel), full of wisdom, perfect in beauty, blameless, and a model of perfection (Ezek 28:11-15). How did such a wonderful creature fall from grace? God asserts through Ezekiel:

> Your heart became proud
> > on account of your beauty,
> and you corrupted your wisdom
> > because of your splendor. (v. 17)

The prophet Isaiah incorporates the same progression by first focusing on the demise of the human king of Babylon and then moving on to the equal demise of an angelic being referred to as the "morning star" (Is 14:12). We quickly learn that the same arrogance that brought down the king of Babylon equally undid Satan.

> You said in your heart,
> > "I will ascend to heaven;
> I will raise my throne
> > above the stars of God." (v. 13)

What most characterizes Satan's sin is the bold assertion "I will," which occurs five times in the space of two verses.[11]

From these two prophets, we can ascertain the following concerning Satan. First, Satan exhibits strong signs of personality, such as intellect, jealousy, and ambition. Second, as a cherub—an angel who has unique access to the throne of God—Satan continually stood in the presence of a flawless God worthy of eternal praise and admiration. Over time, admiration turned to searing jealousy: *Why can't I sit on the throne? Why can't I receive worship? Why can't this all be mine?* Having spent so much time before God, Satan must have been haunted by two facts: this can *never* be all mine and any attempt to possess it will have disastrous results. Yet it did not curb his insatiable desire.

J. R. R. Tolkien, in his classic fantasy books *The Hobbit* and *The Lord of the Rings*, gives us a creative look into where unchecked desire can lead. Readers are introduced to an unsightly character, Gollum, whose life has been destroyed by his unyielding desire to possess the One Ring. While seemingly an ordinary gold ring, this particular ring yields magical powers strong enough to subdue entire kingdoms. However, the one who wields the power of the ring falls prey to its spell. Wizards are wise to warn inhabitants of Middle Earth to avoid its seductive power. Gollum ignores this advice, spending his entire life pathetically trying to possess the ring, which he affectionately names "my precious." Gollum is not ignorant of the dire cost of obtaining the ring. For every year he possesses it, he is transformed from being an innocent hobbit to a deformed and sickly creature controlled by obsession to keep the ring. Though possession of the ring is killing him, he cannot stop his tragic pursuit. Eventually, his final doom is sealed as he risks everything to secure the ring. Similarly, Satan knows he cannot ultimately usurp God and possess his throne, yet he gives up heavenly privilege and position in order to feed his failed obsession, resulting in severe judgment.

 The fact that Satan was once a type of angel called cherubim (plural of cherub) made his betrayal even more tragic. Cherubim were tasked with proclaiming and protecting God's glory and holiness and are pictured as forming God's personal chariot (Ps 18:10). They had four wings and shined like burnished bronze. Ironically, after Satan deceived Adam and Eve into sinning, cherubim protected the gate of the Garden of Eden to keep sinful humans—and perhaps Satan—from coming back to eat from the Tree of Life. Many Jewish writers believed that eating from the tree would keep humans in a perpetual state of sin. Thus, in an act of mercy, God placed cherubim—armed with flaming swords—to keep humans away (Gen 3:24).

SATAN'S JUDGMENT

In candid language, Scripture informs us of the forcefulness of God's judgment. Not only is Satan stripped of his position, but he is cast out of heaven (Is 14:12; Ezek 28:18). Where did he go? The answer has deep implications not only for humans in general but ultimately your marriage specifically. Satan was banished to our planet. However, he did not go without a fight.

The Scriptures introduce us to this cosmic struggle with these chilling words, "Then war broke out in heaven" (Rev 12:7). Using powerful imagery, John describes a cosmic battle in which an enormous red dragon (Satan) flanked with rebelling angels fights against the archangel Michael and his angels. While we do not know how long this battle ensued, John tells us that Satan "was not strong enough," and the dragon and his defeated angels "lost their place in heaven" (Rev 12:8) and were hurled to earth (Rev 12:9). These outcast angels are what New Testament writers call *demons*. How many fell with Satan? John suggests that one-third of the angels were swept up in this failed coup d'état (Rev 12:4). However, not all were allowed to accompany Satan. In an attempt to protect us, God consigned some angels, or demons, directly to hell (2 Pet 2:4). These quarantined demons were "apparently too depraved and harmful to be allowed to roam upon the earth."[12] What do we know about the demons free to wreak havoc on earth?

UNMASKING DEMONS

While we often think of demons as all-powerful beings who delight in terrorizing us, the Scriptures give clear limitations to what they can do. First, demons can only be in one place at a time. In the Gospels, Jesus encounters two men who are afflicted by demons (Mt 8:28-34). When Jesus casts the demons out of the two men, the demons immediately find a home in a herd of pigs. Apparently, they could not be in both the men and pigs. Second, demons excel at observing us but cannot read our minds. After twenty-six years of marriage it only *appears* my wife can read my mind. After years of observing my habits, she can eerily predict what I am going to do or what I am thinking. The same is true of demons who are intently studying us. After careful and consistent study of us, they have a strong understanding of our habits and tendencies. But is it possible they can actually know our thoughts? No. The Scriptures are clear that the only being who is omniscient is God (Ps 139). Third, while demons are powerful, they have limitations. Mark tells us that a man indwelled by demons was able to break free of chains and no one could contain him (Mk 5:3-4). However, unlike God, there are limits to their power. John notes that they cannot do God's work (Jn 10:21) or possess a follower of Jesus.[13]

While demons inherently have these limitations, the Scriptures are clear that they can inflict disease (Lk 13:11), tempt us (1 Thess 3:5), encourage disobedience (Eph 2:2), and, most alarmingly, plant thoughts in our mind (Gen 3:1-5; 2 Cor 4:4; 2 Cor 11:3). In upcoming chapters, we will dive deeper into the strategies of demons and how to utilize spiritual resources to rebuff them.

READER   Stop! Before we go further, I have a million questions.

AUTHOR   I'm not used to being interrupted, but I understand this might all be a little confusing.

READER   Ya think?

AUTHOR   I could do without the sarcasm, but go on.

READER   If God was willing—and able—to send some demons directly to hell, then why didn't he send *all* of them? And while we're at it, why didn't he just send Satan directly to hell? Or even better, why in the world does God create Satan *in the first place!*

AUTHOR   Good questions. Let's start with the easy one: Why did God create Satan?

READER   That's the *easy* one? You gotta be kidding. Well, go for it.

AUTHOR   God didn't create Satan.

READER   What? I thought God created everything?

AUTHOR   He did. What God originally created was a majestic
angel called the *morning star*! This angel had unique
access to God and witnessed firsthand his glory!
This angel also had something you possess, as evidenced by your interrupting me.

READER   What's that?

AUTHOR   Free will. Thus, this angel had a choice to make—do
I continue to worship God, or try to wrestle God's
glory from him? Tragically, he chose rebellion and
became God's adversary or, as we know him, Satan.
But he wasn't created that way.

READER   Couldn't God have forced Satan to continue to
worship him?

AUTHOR   Yes, but what good is forced worship or, for that
matter, forced love? If you knew your friends were
grudgingly manipulated into liking you, wouldn't
that diminish the friendship?

READER   Yes. I don't want people to be forced into liking or
spending time with me.

AUTHOR   God agrees. Therefore, he didn't compel the morning
star or his angels to worship him. They chose rebellion
over praise.

READER   Okay. But why not throw all their "you know whats"
into hell and be done with it?

AUTHOR   Now we are onto the harder question. Why hurl Satan to earth where he had access to Adam and Eve?

READER   You have my attention.

AUTHOR   Like Satan and his angels, God didn't want to force this first couple to follow him. If the only voice Adam and Eve had to listen to was God's, then what choice did they have? Suppose I tell you that you are free to leave a particular room whenever you want. Yet, when you try to leave, every door or window is locked. What would be your response?

READER   Thanks for giving me an option I can't use. Everything's locked. I'm stuck.

AUTHOR   That's right. God didn't want Adam and Eve to be *stuck* with him. So, in the middle of paradise he put an exit door—the tree of the knowledge of good and evil. God was clear. Eating from the tree will have disastrous effects, such as spiritual and physical death. And God allowed Satan access to this couple to be a countervoice—"You will certainly not die" (Gen 3:4). Well, you know the rest.

READER   It seems like God is really committed to us choosing to love him.

AUTHOR   He is. It's a key part of being human. This entire book is about choosing to put God first in our marriages and rebuffing Satan's attempt to derail us. Now may I continue?

READER   Yes. For now.[14]

 If God is committed to humans and angels choosing to love him, then will we have the ability to choose in heaven? If so, couldn't we rebel all over again? The answer is yes and no. Yes, we'll retain free will in heaven, but we won't choose rebellion for several reasons. First, in heaven we'll clearly see sin for all of its ugliness. The attractiveness of sin—so prevalent in this world—will be removed, and our eyes will be open to the full destructiveness of sin. Second, in this life we are constantly putting to death our desire for sin (Col 3:5). In heaven, the desire for holiness is finally consummated. The question "Can we sin in heaven?" presumes that the desire to sin remains in us. In God's full presence that desire will have been once and for all put to death.

As we close this examination of Satan, it is important to remember one key fact. While Satan is God's adversary, he is *not* God's equal. "There are dozens of references to God in the Scriptures for every one to the figure of Satan," notes Christian author John Ortberg. "This reflects a sometimes forgotten theological truth that the devil is by no means God's counterpart. He is a creature, not the Creator."[15] When compared to God, Satan's inferiority becomes pronounced. While Satan can only be in one location at a time, God is everywhere (Ps 139:7-18; Ps 11:4); Satan's knowledge is limited to what he can observe, while God knows everything (Is 46:9-10; Col 2:2-3); Satan's strength is impressive, yet God's strength knows no limits (Job 42:2; Eph 3:20). However, just because God's power dwarfs Satan's, it would be a mistake to think the battle between God and Satan isn't real.

Daniel 10 shows us the reality of this cosmic struggle. In this disturbing chapter, we learn that the prophet Daniel is growing increasingly discouraged because he has fasted and prayed for three weeks for divine help but has received none. Suddenly, an angel appears and informs him that he was dispatched by God after Daniel's *first* prayer but was delayed because "the prince of the Persian kingdom resisted me twenty-one days" (vv. 12-13). The angel eventually broke through demonic resistance only when the archangel Michael showed up to fight with him (v. 13). While this passage is filled with mystery and must be interpreted with care, we can ascertain certain insights. First, while God's superiority was never in doubt, at times demonic resistance can hinder his angels and our prayers. Second, if the fight is real for angels like Michael, then we can be assured the fight is equally real for us. Third, even though Satan is inferior, he can still win significant victories.

Not only is Satan God's inferior, he is a defeated creature. The Scriptures assure us that Satan's fate is sealed—he will one day be forever banished in exile. Using vivid language, John assures his readers that Satan—and all those who willingly followed him—will be "thrown" into a lake of fire, where they will be forced to face the consequences of their rebellion "day and night" for eternity (Rev 20:10). However, followers of Christ live in the reality that this final banishment has yet to occur. Our enemy is desperate, wounded, and looking for a fight.

Toward the end of 1944, German armies were in tatters and Hitler was fortifying himself in Berlin. While the final result of the war was no longer in doubt, it mattered little to soldiers defending the Third Reich. Some of the conflicts at the end of the war—such as the Battle of the Bulge—were the fiercest fought. Why? German soldiers, facing certain defeat, still bitterly fought to defend their homeland. In fact, some of Hitler's most hardened troops continued to fight for weeks after Germany officially surrendered on May 7, 1945. The same is true of our battle with Satan. The Scriptures tell us that the earth is Satan's domain (1 Jn 5:19), and though he knows he'll eventually lose, he still fiercely defends his territory. Peter, when describing this beaten angelic foe, stated he is a "roaring lion" seeking to devour those around him (1 Pet 5:8). Peter intentionally used graphic language to grab our attention and prod us into preparing for likely attacks.

CONTINUING THE CONVERSATION

1. What images do you associate with Satan or the devil? List five descriptors of the devil that readily come to mind. Are these images spurred on by the Scriptures or pop culture?

2. While most of the global church takes Satan seriously, the church in the West struggles to embrace the reality of spiritual battle. Why? When you think through the last year, how many sermons did you hear about Satan or spiritual battle? Why does the uncomfortable idea of spiritual battle cause Western Christians to shy away from the reality of Satan?

3. What keeps you as a couple from embracing the reality of spiritual battle? How often do you or your friends discuss Satan or the possibility of spiritual opposition?

2

WHY WOULD SATAN CARE ABOUT MY MARRIAGE?

Sarah is an ordinary waitress working at a hole-in-the-wall restaurant. In addition to her regular customers, she notices a stranger hanging around. Dressed in a black leather jacket and wearing dark sunglasses, he never enters but stares through the storefront window. It is becoming more difficult for Sarah to pass it off as coincidence. Unexpectedly, one morning the stranger comes into the restaurant, seemingly hiding something behind his back. Suddenly, he pulls out a pump shotgun and starts shooting—at her! As she runs out the back of the restaurant, he follows with murderous intent. *Why is he after me? Why single me out? What have I done?* her thoughts scream at her as she narrowly escapes.

Over time, Sarah learns that she is the target of a futuristic cyborg assassin intent on killing her. Why? She comes to understand—along with millions of fans of the 1984 sci-fi classic *The Terminator*—that in the near future the human race will be nearly extinct at the hands of hostile hyperintelligent machines. However, humans will successfully lead a rebellion against the machines orchestrated by an unlikely leader—Sarah Connor. To stop the rebellion, the machines send a robot (played by Arnold Schwarzenegger, "I'll be back!") into the past to stop the rebellion *before* it starts, and Sarah realizes her importance! For those unfamiliar with *The Terminator* franchise, the plot may seem wildly unrealistic: a waitress leading a human rebellion against high-tech cyborg assassins? What is she going to do—throw tip money at them?

Ironically, the Scriptures offer a plot that seems equally unlikely. Earth has been deeply influenced by a sinister angelic being and his horde of rebellious followers. We learn that this angelic force has influenced entire countries and world systems. What is God's response? In an unlikely move, God assumes human form and personally leads an invasion force to free earth. In an unexpected twist that foreshadows *The Terminator*, he chooses to come not as a military or political leader but rather as a carpenter from a nondescript hole-in-the-wall place called Nazareth. God's invasion force is not made up of the religious elite but rather ordinary farmers, peasants, fishers, and even ostracized tax gatherers. In other words, it consists of Sarah Connor types who have yet to realize their importance but are targets nonetheless. How do our marriages fit in God's invasion plans? The answer becomes clear when we learn what motivates Satan's rebellion toward God.

THE FINAL STRAW

When I was growing up, my family played a game called "The Last Straw Camel." It is a simple game where, based on the cards you get, you need to put plastic straws onto the back of a toy camel. If you are the unlucky person who puts *one too many* straws on the camel's back and it breaks in two—you lose. Apparently, Satan was involved in his own version of "Last Straw Camel" with God. What were the perceived indignities (straws) that pushed Satan over the edge toward cosmic rebellion? As stated in chapter one, as a cherub Satan had unique access to the throne of God and was tasked with bestowing onto God the praise he rightfully deserved. What started to wear on Satan was the fact that he did not have his own throne or domain he could rule by himself (Is 14:13). Over time, his desire to be above God started to grow. However, what was the *last straw* that pushed the morning star to become God's adversary (Satan)? Surprisingly, it was the creation of us! The special status given to humans was the final slight.

King David, in reflecting on God's special love for humans, gives us keen insight into the many straws that fueled Satan's jealousy. In quick succession, David lays out factors that pulled at Satan's ego. First, while David acknowledges all the works of God (heavens, moon, stars) he is amazed that God is more mindful of humans than galaxies. He writes, "What is mankind that you are mindful of them, human beings that you care for them?" (Ps 8:4). These two terms *mindful* and *care* reveal much about God's affection for us. The Hebrew word *mindful* comes from the root *zkr*, which connotes a person tenderly remembering another person. On the screen saver of my laptop, I have a photo of my three boys standing shoulder to shoulder. Each time I fire up my computer the photo calls to mind my affection for each one of them. The same is true of God's tender awareness of us. The word *care* comes from the root *pqd*, which can mean seeking out or longing for a person. Old Testament scholar Gerald Wilson concludes, "It is as if God's calling to mind his human creatures sparks such a longing for them that he must seek them out and lavish care on them."[1] How much did God's care and mindfulness of human creatures start to weigh on Satan?

Another perceived slight or straw was the exalted position God gives to humans. David states that God made us a "little lower than the angels and crowned them with glory and honor" (Ps 8:5). Humans, though frail, are in God's estimation a *little lower* than angelic beings that reside in the heavens.[2] In addition, we are crowned with glory and honor. In the Near Eastern world, kings showed special status to others by bestowing them with crowns. Astonishingly, David says that we are crowned with *glory*—the same Hebrew word (*kabod*) often used of God himself. In other words, when God looks at us, he sees aspects of his own glory. In his classic *The Screwtape Letters*, C. S. Lewis imagines how a demon would respond to God's love for mortals. Screwtape, a senior devil, is disgusted that "this animal, this thing begotten in a bed" could look upon God and find such intimate favor![3]

Another significant straw is that God made us "ruler over the works" of his hands and put "everything under [our] feet" (Ps 8:6). God has set humans apart "by the glory and honor of his image, so he also sets apart humans by giving them responsibility over the earth."[4] We have been given a world—already deemed good by God—to exercise dominion. A place of our own that brings great responsibility, privilege, and honor.

To summarize, Satan's great longing was to have glory on par with God and have a place in the cosmos that he could call his own—a place where he could have dominion and transform others into his own image. How much of an affront was it when he learned that humans are not only the objects of God's care but are essentially on the same level as angelic beings, and that humans—not Satan—are to be given a place to govern? The result of so many perceived slights stirred up an incorrigible rebellion against God. In defeat, Satan was banished from heaven to earth. What has he been doing since?

The Scriptures inform us that angels have great interest in the affairs of humans. One aspect of particular interest is God's willingness to sacrifice his own Son to save rebellious humans. Peter writes that concerning this area "even angels long to look into these things" (1 Pet 1:12). The verb *parakypto*, "long to look," means to "stoop over to look" and suggests intense exploration rather than a glance. However, what sparked joy for some angels no doubt infuriated others. Is it possible that for fallen angels (demons) God's pursuit of sinful humans was an act that solidified their rebellion? *They sin and yet God still loves them! They rebel and God still sends his Son to save them! Why are they so special?*

SATAN'S MYTHS ABOUT MARRIAGE

Written in fifth century BC, *The Art of War* is considered one of the definitive books on battle tactics. The author, Sun Tzu, devotes thirteen chapters to the diverse aspects of war. The most important chapter, however, is not devoted to weapons, leadership, or morale, but rather to *terrain*. Sun Tzu asserts that battles are won or lost due to who controls the terrain (such as, who secures the high ground). If the terrain does not suit your purposes, then change it to fit your strategy (uproot trees, dam up water sources, create your own high ground using raw materials). Apparently, Satan has taken a page out of *The Art of War*.

Since being banished from heaven and cast to earth, Satan has been changing the terrain to fit his purposes. But how? The Scriptures give us a clue when John shockingly asserts, "the whole world is under the control of the evil one" (1 Jn 5:19). New Testament scholar Clint Arnold unpacks this alarming statement. Arnold explains that for John the "world" refers to "human society in terms of its organized opposition to God" and extends to "human institutions and organizations, the social and political order."[5] In other words, Satan is changing the terrain of our world, in part by deeply influencing how our culture thinks about God, sex, marriage, love, money, and so on. Keep in mind that "culture is nothing more than the constant and curious conversation that goes on between every one of us and the environment in which we reside—we ourselves being part of that environment."[6]

The following observations give us a clue as to how Satan has attempted to influence our conversations about key issues by molding the cultural ground we stand on. While the list is not exhaustive, it helps us understand how Satan's goal is not only to solidify his opposition to God but to weaken human relationships in the process.

Marriage as a contract. Over time, most Americans have adopted a contractual view of marriage as a legal obligation. As in any contract, two parties agree to fulfill their part of the agreement. If one party breaks the contract or violates a key aspect of it, the entire contract is null and void. Bob Larkin, writing for *Men's Health* magazine, boldly states, "The secret to long-term happiness is simple: think of your marriage as a transaction."[7] However, what happens when the transaction goes bad?

Last summer we had our house painted. In advance, we agreed with the painter on the quality and color of paint, rain contingencies, and deadline. A contract was signed and down payment given. When the job was completed, we walked around the house to inspect the quality. It was then we noticed that the painter had used a different shade of white—who knew there were so many varieties—from what we wanted. Our response? We withheld the final payment until he fulfilled his obligation. Welcome to American marriage.

Many couples today operate under an assumption of *you do your part and I'll do mine.* However, what happens when one spouse feels the other is not doing their part? And what if I feel I am doing *more* than you? An old adage states, *a person who says he'll meet you halfway is often a poor judge of distance.* Psychologists note that a fundamental mistake we make in judging others is that we are biased toward the quality and amount we think we put into relationships. In other words, from my perspective I'm always doing *more*! In a contractual view of marriage couples are always evaluating each other and, in many cases, conclude their spouse is not meeting them halfway. Over time, disappointment takes over and individuals look for a way out.

David Popenoe, a social researcher at Rutgers University, notes that marriage used to be a bond of mutual dependency rooted in extended families and a "religious bond of sacramental worth." He offers a chilling assessment of the current state of marriage: "Marriage has become a purely individual pursuit; an implied and not very enforceable contract between two people, a relationship designed to satisfy basic needs for intimacy, dependency and sex. When these needs change, or when a presumptively better partner is discovered, marriages are easily dissolved."[8]

Multitasking marriages. I sit in front of our television with my laptop open. As I occasionally glance at the TV, I switch from responding to emails to checking out the latest sports scores to breaking news updates. In today's multitasking world, I've grown comfortable working on many projects simultaneously. My wife walks into the room and asks if she can get my input. I close my laptop and mute the TV. "Sure," I respond. As she speaks I quickly find my attention wandering toward half-written emails or the buzzing of my cell phone in my pocket. I offer a quick response and suggest we talk later. I eagerly return to unfinished tasks. I justify my distraction by promising to myself that when we further discuss her concern, she'll have my *full* attention. Not so fast, suggests researchers.

Clifford Nass, a professor of communication at Stanford who studies human attentiveness, asserts that continually switching between multiple tasks can hinder your ability to monotask (focus on one thing). He explains, "We have scales that allow us to divide up people into people who multitask all the time and people who rarely do, and the differences are remarkable. People who multitask all the time can't filter out irrelevancy. They can't manage a working memory. They're chronically distracted."[9]

In other words, my assumption that when my wife and I do resume our conversation I'll be able to give her my full attention may be a promise I can't easily fulfill. Through regular multitasking am I losing the ability to focus on one thing or person? Nass concludes that through multitasking we "train our brains to a new way of thinking. And then when we try to revert our brains back, our brains are plastic but they're not elastic. They don't just snap back into shape."[10]

A disturbing result surfaces from our proclivity toward multitasking. People who regularly multitask begin to see all distractions as carrying the same weight or significance.[11] In other words, the distraction of a spouse is on equal footing as the distraction of responding to unread emails. Our ability to recognize or give preference to important issues is slowly compromised.

Romantic love can complete us. In 1995 Match.com was launched. Many scoffed at the notion of finding your soul mate via a website. Today, Match.com is in twenty-five different countries with no signs of slowing down. While Match.com may be the most popular dating website, they are hardly alone, with eHarmony, Elite Singles, Zoosk, ProfessionalMatch, and Christian Singles all gaining ground. In fact, more than 2,500 services and apps now exist with 70 percent of American singles using them.[12] While some users are merely looking for casual relationships or hooking up, many are driven by the desire to finally obtain a love that will fulfill them.

Regardless of that newest romantic comedy—*The Big Sick, Home Again, Entanglement*—all of my students can quote word-for-word lines from two iconic movies that have most shaped how they view love. In the movie *Jerry Maguire*, a love-struck sports agent (Tom Cruise) *finally* realizes he is in love with a single mom (Renee Zellweger) and decides to crash a gathering of her and her friends. As he bursts through the door, he utters a line known by millions of forlorn lovers: "You complete me!" To which she responds, "You had me at hello."

Romantic films also carry the message that the person who will complete you may be drastically *different* from you. One year after *Jerry Maguire*, the epic movie *Titanic* was released. In addition to telling the story of the ill-fated voyage of the RMS *Titanic*, it introduced audiences to the unlikely romance between seventeen-year-old Rose DeWitt (a first-class passenger engaged to a millionaire) and Jack Dawson (a penniless artist). Standing on the bow of the boat, with Jack securely holding her, Rose proclaims, "I'm flying!" They quickly fall passionately in love, consummate their budding relationship in the back seat of a car parked in storage, and dream of the future.

"Jack, when this boat docks I'm getting off with you!" Rose announces.

"This is crazy!" Jack responds.

"I know," proclaims Rose. "It makes no sense. That's why I trust it!"

What? Where will they go? How will they pay the bills? Can you really live off of love? Yes, conclude millions of star-crossed young lovers sitting in darkened auditoriums.

Are movies like *Jerry Maguire* or *Titanic* merely harmless romantic fantasies? Researchers at Heriot Watt University in Edinburgh sought to determine if a steady diet of consuming romantic fictions could negatively influence how we view love, sex, and marriage. Their conclusion: watching films such as *Jerry Maguire* or

Titanic can ruin your love life by creating wildly unrealistic expectations that no person or relationship can fulfill.[13]

 A pivotal moment in Christ's temptation in the wilderness is when Satan takes him to the top of a mountain and shows him all the kingdoms of the world and their splendor. "All this I give you," states Satan, "if you will bow down and worship me" (Mt 4:9). It is important to note several factors. First, in an attempt to deceive Christ, Satan presents earthly kingdoms "in all their glory" (Mt. 4:8) with human sin conveniently glossed over—a façade of what they really are. Second, while Jesus rejects his offer, he does not challenge Satan's authority to give him the kingdoms. Jesus recognizes that the power structures of the world fall under his temporary governance. Paul concurs with Jesus' assessment when he labels Satan as the "god of this age" (2 Cor 4:4).

CHRISTIAN MARRIAGE: RECLAIMING LOST TERRAIN

If Satan's purpose is to help create cultural terrain that reflects his priorities, then a purpose of your marriage is to counter his priorities by modeling values rooted in God's kingdom. In short, we offer a vibrant alternative to the world around us.

In a fifty-four-block area in downtown Los Angeles, over seventeen thousand homeless people try to live with some sense of dignity. Trying to secure dignity—let alone keep warm, find food, practice hygiene—is almost impossible since there are only nine public restrooms that can be used by inhabitants once stores or restaurants close. Over time this area came to be infamously known as *skid row*. The term is barrowed from loggers who would send tree trunks down river to collect at a waiting area where logs slammed into each other. Similarly, skid row is a massive collection of people who have been either abandoned by health care providers or try to find security in numbers. Thousands of people slammed into each other with little resources. What hope do they have?

In the heart of skid row is a five-story, 225,000 square-foot facility that has become a sanctuary. The Union Rescue Mission is the largest private homeless shelter in the United States and provides food, shelter, clothing, medical assistance, education, job training, and spiritual direction for all who walk through its doors. Most importantly, the mission restores dignity. Concerning the woeful lack of public restrooms for the homeless, the director of the mission, Andy Bales, states "We should not let any human being experience that kind of embarrassment or indignity or shame of having to utilize a sidewalk for a restroom, let alone live in the filth."[14]

Bales is simply reflecting the heart of the mission's founder. The mission was started in the 1800s by oil businessman Lyman Stewart, who wanted to give a physical representation to God's love and provision. In short, a community that helped people not only survive but flourish. Theologian Rick Langer observes that Christian communities such as the Union Rescue Mission serve as "an outpost for the kingdom—a foretaste of heaven."[15] Lyman Stewart was simply following the Scripture's admonition to exhibit "good lives" among others that "they may see your good deeds and glorify God" (1 Pet 2:12). As Jesus reminds us, "a town built on a hill cannot be hidden" (Mt 5:14).

MARRIAGE AS AN OUTPOST
FOR GOD'S KINGDOM

While encouraging, what do rescue missions have to do with my marriage? In a world where the fingerprints of Satan are everywhere, we offer marriages that reclaim enemy-occupied territory by being outposts for a different kingdom. In being countercultural, our marriages operate under a different set of values. These values, if applied, not only help marriages flourish but restore a sense of dignity originally bestowed by God. The following are ways we can reclaim relational territory.

Marriage as covenant. In a culture where marriage is seen as a contract, we live out relationships that are covenantal. One of the most well-known covenants, the Declaration of Independence, concludes: "And for the support of this Declaration, with a firm reliance on the protection of divine Providence, we mutually pledge to each other our Lives, our Fortunes and our sacred Honor." Notice two features of this covenant. First, it is a pledge to others that is *not* voided if the other person does not follow through. Second, the ability to follow through rests squarely on God's providence or strength. In the same way, covenantal marriages pledge fidelity to each other even if one spouse does not keep up their end. And most importantly, the marriage draws strength from God—not merely from each other. In short, spouses in a covenant marriage bear with each other, and forgiveness is given not based on merit but as a natural overflow of Christ's enduring love (Col 3:13).

Focused marriages. Today, spouses engage in fevered multitasking in an attempt to do *more.* Each day bleeds into another producing fatigue, anxiety, and restlessness. Christian marriages—rooted in

Sabbath rest—seek to regularly break the pull of culture. Theologian
Walter Brueggemann states that Sabbath is restraint. He notes that
Sabbath is "an antidote to anxiety that both derives from our craving
and in turn feeds those cravings for more. Sabbath is an arena in
which to recognize that we live by gift and not by possession, that we
are satisfied by relationships of attentive fidelity and not by amassing
commodities."[16] Spouses seeking to love each other according to biblical principles—putting others' needs above our own, loving uncon-
ditionally, offering undivided attention—keenly understand that they
need to rest deeply in God's love, grace, and provision. As the psalmist
suggests, strength is found in being *still* (Ps 46:10).

In today's multitasking culture, Christian couples need to learn
to be *still* by placing priority on their spouse's needs and learn to
give focused attention to each other. To use Nass's terminology, we
need to retrain our brains to focus on what is important. A key way
of determining what is important is cultivating Sabbath rest, where
we focus on God's priorities. The result is a deep reservoir of God's
grace from which we can draw to extend grace and focused attention to one another.

Only God can fulfill. Regardless of what romantic movies
promise, Christians understand that no imperfect human spouse
or child can give us what we long for—pure, unconditional love.
In his *Confessions*, Augustine wisely notes that only God's love can
fulfill us. He writes, "You have made us for yourself, and our hearts
are restless, until they can find rest in you."[17] Only after rooting
ourselves in God's perfect love will we be able to accept the highs
and lows of human love. Simply put, I do not expect my spouse to
love me in ways only God can.

Why is my marriage a target? Like the Union Rescue Mission, which serves as a vibrant alternative to the inhabitants of skid row, we too offer glimpses to our neighbors of what a covenant marriage can look like when modeled after kingdom priorities. Every time our marriage reflects God's values, we take back a little of the terrain shaped by human rebellion goaded by spiritual influences. Yet being countercultural comes with potential risk.

 If, as the Scriptures state, the whole world is in the power of the evil one, then is all of culture bad? No. In his compassion, God has infused the world with what theologians call common grace. Common grace means that concepts of goodness, beauty, compassion, courage, justice, and love are available to all. Thus, non-Christian EMS workers, civic leaders, teachers, doctors, politicians, and so on can do much good in society. Christians need to affirm the good of culture, while resisting the aspects that stray from God's kingdom.

PAUL'S ENCOURAGEMENT AND WARNING

In Paul's letter to the church at Ephesus he reminds us that as followers of Christ we were formerly in "darkness" but now walk as "children of light" (Eph 5:8). In the past, we bought into a cultural terrain sculpted in part by spiritual forces at war against God. However, we now exhibit lives that give others a glimpse into a new type of terrain saturated with God's love. A key way we show others God's love, asserts Paul, is through our marriages.

Toward the end of his letter, Paul gives an in-depth look into how Christian marriages work. While there is much Paul addresses—sexual purity, removing coarse talk, yielding to the Sprit, submitting to each other, marital headship—it is crucial to focus on the *motivation* to do what Paul commands. As a husband, I am called to love my wife "just as Christ loved the church and gave himself up for her" (Eph 5:25). My motivation is rooted in how Christ loves me. Paul insists, notes theologian A. Skevington Wood, that "the love of a Christian man for his wife must be a response to and an expression of the love of God in Christ extended to the church."[18] In other words, my motivation to love and sacrifice for my wife—in contrast to a contractual view of marriage—is not based on her being lovable or even loving me. I love as Christ loved me.

The same applies to my wife, who is called to respect and affirm me "out of reverence for Christ" (Eph 5:21). The Greek word for "reverence" means to venerate or treat with deference. My wife's respect for me or willingness to follow my lead is not motivated by my actions but by her deep reverence for her Savior. This is not to suggest that a wife must blindly follow a husband who abandons her, is abusive, or tries to lead her into sin. By his sinful decisions a Christian husband can abdicate his role and authority.

The motivation described by Paul that fuels a Christian husband and wife stands in stark contrast to our culture's "I'll do my part, you do yours" approach to marriage. Once our motivation has been addressed, Paul prepares us for significant struggles that lie ahead.

After Paul completes his vision for Christian marriage he then launches into his plea that we all "put on the full armor of God" so we can "stand against the devil's schemes" (Eph 6:11). In Paul's original letters there were no chapter breaks. Thus, his discussion of marriage and spiritual battle are not separated but are one continuous thought. The message could not be clearer—to build your marriage on biblical principles will entail spiritual battle since our struggle is not against "flesh and blood" but "against the powers of this dark world" (Eph 6:12).

What does this struggle against spiritual forces look like in daily life? How can I tell if the argument with my spouse is just a matter of difference of opinion or something being spurred on by spiritual forces? In chapter three we will consider practical ways to diagnose the demonic.

INTERVIEW: DISCUSSING SPIRITUAL BATTLE

Joanne Jung is a gifted professor, writer, and mentor of students. However, her passion is being a wife, mother, and grandmother. She takes seriously the idea that evil forces may be targeting her marriage, children, and grandchildren. Often what keeps couples from talking with each other or their children about Satan and spiritual battle is confusion as to how to bring up the subject. How do we discuss Satan without freaking out each other or the kids? Joanne has found an unlikely source of wisdom for discussing spiritual topics of all kinds—the English Puritans.[19] How can the insight of Puritans help us discuss the thorny reality of spiritual battle?

TIM   You have found a source of wisdom that can help spouses or parents create an environment to discuss spiritual topics of all kinds. What drew you to the Puritans for guidance?

JOANNE   The Puritans were passionate about two ideas. First, they had an amazingly high view of Scripture. Scripture served as a litmus test for their lives. Second, they were deeply concerned with how we can live out what the Bible says in practical ways. Puritans would often say to each other, "How stands it now between God and your soul?"

TIM   I was going to ask you that at the start of our conversation, but it slipped my mind.

JOANNE   (chuckling) Maybe next time.

TIM   How did Puritans try to apply what they were learning by reading God's Word or what they heard in a sermon?

JOANNE   After a sermon, they would gather together as a family or with a small group of friends and break out notes they'd taken and discuss it. They called this type of gathering *conferencing*.

TIM   Can you elaborate?

JOANNE   Conferencing was a rhythm of having spiritual conversations that were informed by biblical truths. The goal was to care for another person by asking well-framed questions that would nudge people to a greater understanding of God, the things of God, and one another.

TIM   Conferencing was a regular part of family life for Puritans?

JOANNE   Oh, yes! Parents felt a great responsibility to engage children through guided family discussions that sought to take the Bible seriously. They didn't wait for a pastor or youth director to influence their children. A great responsibility for spiritual growth lay within the home. Parents took seriously the command to teach children in the home while eating, doing chores, or relaxing (Deut 6:5-9). Puritans referred to their families as *little churches*.

TIM   How might that look today? How can parents use the idea of conferencing to discuss spiritual warfare?

JOANNE   Well, they might call the family together and say something like: "As your parents, we want to take the Bible seriously. To do so entails taking the idea of the devil and spiritual warfare seriously. In your own reading, you see how often Jesus addresses this topic. What should we do as a family to follow his example? What would it look like to live out what Jesus believed?"

TIM   So it's a guided discussion, not a lengthy parental sermon? I'm pretty good at those!

JOANNE   It's easy to slip into giving sermons to our children. The goal of conferencing is to spur each other's thinking about how biblical issues intersect with life. You are not just shooting the breeze or giving lengthy speeches. As a family, you are asking how a biblical topic—such as spiritual warfare—applies to daily life. The great thing about conferencing is that you don't have to be a Bible expert to ask good questions.

TIM   How would such a meeting end?

JOANNE   Perhaps in prayer. "What if, as a family, we regularly prayed that the Holy Spirit would make it known to all of us how the devil might be trying to derail our family?" At the next family meeting everyone could share what the Spirit revealed.

TIM   So, this is for everyone, not just the kids.

JOANNE   Children need to see parents working on their own
              spirituality, allowing God's Spirit to be manifested in
              them. Conferencing is about the entire family!

TIM   One last question. What if readers have young children?
              How do you bring up spiritual warfare without causing
              nightmares?

JOANNE   We definitely want to be sensitive to young ears.
              Perhaps as we sing that familiar song "This Little Light
              of Mine," we could draw attention to one key part.

TIM   Refresh my memory.

JOANNE   "This little light of mine, I'm gonna let it shine." And
              the second verse, "Don't let Satan poof it out." This
              way, we are slowly introducing the topic to children.
              Later, we can explore how Satan attempts to extin-
              guish our light or passion for Christ.

TIM   It sounds like the Puritans have made an impact on you.

JOANNE   (smiling) I call them some of my best old dead friends.

CONTINUING THE CONVERSATION

1. What difference does it make to adopt a covenant view of
   marriage (unconditional fidelity to a spouse) as opposed to
   a contractual view (evaluating each other to see if a spouse
   is fulfilling his or her end of relationship)? How might a
   covenant view foster grace toward a spouse?

2. In today's frenetic world of technology and multitasking, what
   might Sabbath rest look like on a weekly basis? What practical
   steps might a couple take to have a weekly technological fast?

3. Only after rooting ourselves in God's perfect love will we be able to accept the highs and lows of human love. In what ways am I expecting my spouse to love me in ways only God can?

4. Applying the Puritan concept of conferencing, how might you structure a family meeting to discuss the reality of spiritual battle? How would you start? Perhaps, start the conversation with this thought-provoking quote by theologian Clint Arnold: "On this topic [the reality of Satan] some of us suffer a double-mindedness. Although mental assent is given to the likelihood that evil spirits exist since it is affirmed in the Bible, in reality it makes no practical difference in the way we live our day-to-day lives."[20]

3

HOW CAN I TELL IF THIS IS SPIRITUAL WARFARE?

What a difference twelve months make.

When they started dating, Ken and Maria knew they were opposites. Ken was an accountant who devoured statistics, and Maria taught elementary school kids and loved the arts. Yet they seemed to balance each other out. He provided organization and predictability, and she loosened him up to be more spontaneous. While none of their friends would have paired them up, it seemed to work in an odd way. Then they got married.

Seeing each other regularly quickly transitioned into living with each other 24/7. Over time, the strengths and quirks that attracted them to each other started to become sources of irritation. Ken mostly loved her endless energy and spontaneity, but was mystified by how she treated their finances. Maria appreciated Ken's bottom-line attitude but increasingly started to feel suffocated. The anger this surfaced surprised both of them. How can two people who love each other go through periods where they didn't want to be in the same room? Slowly, positive thoughts and believing the best about each other morphed into resignation that things will only get worse. *How will we feel about each other in five years?* Maria wondered.

How can Ken and Maria distinguish between the relational bumps inherent in making a transition into marriage and the possible presence of spiritual opposition? Every couple experiences ups and downs in a marriage. But what if you find yourself in a funk that seems to go on and on? What should we look for when marital struggles will not go away and negative thoughts start to spiral? Is it merely marital growing pains or something more? What criteria can we use?

In this chapter we'll take a close look at symptoms or signs of the demonic by considering criteria used by Christians over the centuries, and then focus on specific indicators agreed on by theologians.

TESTING THE SPIRITS

"Dear friends," writes John, "do not believe every spirit, but test the spirits to see whether they are from God" (1 Jn 4:1). A key skill for Christians is learning to discern *who* is seeking to influence them. Specifically, spouses need to be aware of spiritual forces trying to pull them apart or weaken marital harmony.

St. Ignatius of Loyola—an influential church leader of the sixteenth century—created a simple rule to test the spirits, which has guided believers over the centuries. *Does the influence of a spirit move a believer toward the fruit of the Spirit or toward the deeds of the flesh?* Ignatius is referring to a set of lists described by the apostle Paul in his letter to Christians in Galatia. These two lists act like a continuum that assists a couple in determining if they are being tempted to move toward or away from God.

 In 1521, while recovering from a battle wound in Spain's war against the French, Ignatius of Loyola had a dramatic conversion to Christianity. Over time he developed deep insight into how to cultivate intimacy with God, and his book *Spiritual Exercises* is to this day regarded as one of the most influential books on spiritual life ever written.* His legacy is tied to his founding of the Society of Jesus or, as we know them today, the Jesuits.

---

*To read more of these helpful exercises, see George E. Ganes, *The Spiritual Exercises of Saint Ignatius: A Translation and Commentary* (Chicago: Loyola Press, 1992). To see how these exercises can help you understand the impact of sin and temptation, see Larry Warner, *Journey with Jesus: Discovering the Spiritual Exercises of Saint Ignatius* (Downers Grove, IL: InterVarsity Press, 2010).

MOVING TOWARD THE FLESH

Paul begins by describing specific deeds of the flesh that pull at each believer, such as sexual immorality, impurity, debauchery, idolatry, witchcraft, hatred, discord, jealousy, rage, selfish ambition, dissensions, envy, and drunkenness (Gal 5:19-21). Paul's list seems to be broken down into four broad categories that cover sins of a sexual nature, violating religious standards, actions between people that rupture relationships, and concludes with sins common among nonbelievers of his day. Each category has deep implications for couples intent on following God.

 Often when biblical authors use the word *flesh*, they are not merely referring to our physical bodies. Rather, they are describing the part of us still inclined toward the old habits, attitudes, or desires we had as non-Christians. In short, it is the inner conflict we have as believers as we seek to be more like Christ. Even some of the most admired followers of Christ have felt this inward battle. In a candid moment the apostle Paul powerfully states, "I do not understand what I do. For what I want to do I do not do, but what I hate I do" (Rom 7:15).

Sexual sin. Paul uses the term *sexual immorality* to describe the physical act of intercourse outside the marriage. What could lead to such a drastic breaking of fidelity between spouses? *Impurity* connotes a gradual state of becoming unclean in a moral or religious sense. During New Testament times, religious followers were well aware of strict rules governing moral action. Setting aside of those rules resulted in increasing levels of impurity. Finally, Paul uses the word *debauchery* to describe a person who no longer cares about following the rules and lives in open and reckless rebellion. In today's hookup culture of casual sex, movies and prime-time television that celebrate deviating from sexual norms, and the widespread prevalence of pornography, Paul's list of sexual sins is as relevant today as it was in his time. The sexual immorality Paul describes has been on vivid display with the rise of the #MeToo movement drawing attention to sexual assault and harassment all too prevalent in today's society.

Religious sin. In an ancient world of gods and goddesses, Paul defines *idolatry* as giving anything primacy over devotion to the true

God. It is worshiping worldly things—social status, money, love, sex, and material things—rather than worshiping the Creator. *Witchcraft* is the temptation to utilize dark powers to achieve status, power, and possessions. How much has our obsession with achieving the American Dream—always desiring to move up the social ladder—become an idol for couples, resulting in debt, anxiety, and envy?

Relational sin. It is shocking that of the indicators of the flesh mentioned by Paul, over half have to do with harmful interactions with others. When Paul begins his description of the flesh, he states that the "acts of the flesh are obvious" (Gal 5:19). It does not take much explanation to understand how *hatred, jealousy, rage, selfishness,* and *envy* can lead to *discord, dissensions,* and ultimately *factions.* Couples immersed in a social milieu marked by radical individualism (selfishness), social comparison fostered by slick marketing campaigns (jealousy, envy), and hostile disagreements prevalent in social media (hatred, rage) are primed for discord and dissension in their relationships.

Public sin. Paul concludes his list with two public displays of the flesh common to his day—*drunkenness* and *orgies.* Rather than hiding their impurity, many delight in publically displaying a disregard for social norms or God's commands. When considering drunkenness, one can't help but think of many college campuses where drinking to excess is not only the norm but the expectation. Tragically, in the case of the well-documented fraternity hazing incident at Penn State University in 2017 a nineteen-year-old pledge was made to drink eighteen alcoholic drinks in an hour, resulting in his death.[1] With the explosion of pornography through social media, orgies of all kinds are graphically displayed and downloaded. Sadly, we often think the ancient world Paul describes is primitive and debased. Yet modern examples we've considered show us that the same pull toward the flesh is just as prevalent today.

MOVING TOWARD THE SPIRIT

In contrast to the deeds of the flesh, Paul explores what is commonly known as the fruit of the Spirit (Gal 5:22-23). Since "God is love" (1 Jn 4:8), Paul starts his list with the attribute of *love*. Just as God deeply loves us and crowns us with love and compassion (Ps 103:4), we are to treat others in the same way. Consequently, his list describing the fruit of the Spirit (*love, patience, kindness, goodness, self-control,* and *gentleness*) replaces the hatred, jealousy, rage, and selfishness found in the previous list. The result of following the Spirit's lead is a deep-seated *joy*. This joy is not based on the size of our bank account, the success of our careers, or even the health of our marriages. Joy is rooted in God's unchanging love and goodness. From this love, we extend love to others—especially to our imperfect spouses.

WHICH DIRECTION IS YOUR MARRIAGE HEADING?

As you look at Paul's two lists, which most characterizes your marriage? While no relationship is perfect, do descriptors of the flesh outnumber the qualities of the Spirit? Most importantly, what role do spiritual forces play in trying to move you toward the flesh? How are we to interpret St. Ignatius's notion that *any* temptation to move away from God's Spirit should be considered as spiritual warfare? Does that mean that every time I am angry with my spouse or act selfishly or am tempted to look at inappropriate images on the computer I am under spiritual attack? The key to applying Ignatius's rule is to understand what the Scripture's refer to as a "foothold."

New Testament scholar Clint Arnold notes that in Paul's warning to Christians to be careful not to give the devil a foothold (Eph 4:27), the Greek word for foothold (*topos*) can also be translated as *opportunity* or *chance*. Thus, Paul's warning could be translated "do not give the devil a chance to exert his influence."[2] What might be an opportunity the devil could manipulate? Paul answers, "Do not let the sun go down while you are still angry" (Eph 4:26). Our anger—a quality named as a deed of the flesh—is one way we afford the devil an opportunity to exert influence. "For this reason," states Arnold, "it is extremely dangerous for believers to harbor bitterness, hold a grudge, or pilfer from their place of employment." He concludes, "Giving into those temptations does not just confirm the weakness of the flesh, it opens up the lives of believers to the control of the devil and his powers."[3]

An understanding of what constitutes a foothold combined with Ignatius's rule helps create a broad principle for assessing if spiritual attack is happening. *Giving into the deeds of the flesh (e.g., selfishness, anger, impurity) is not in itself spiritual battle. It could merely be old habits coming to the surface. However, choosing not to counteract the deeds of the flesh with fruit of the Spirit (e.g., love, patience, faithfulness) should be considered as giving the devil an opportunity to exert increasing influence, an opportunity he will seek to maximize.*

Understanding St. Ignatius's rule and the concept of footholds provides insight into the early marital struggles of Ken and Maria that opened this chapter. Over time, Ken and Maria started to view the traits that attracted them to each other as irritations. Frequently, they would go to bed increasingly annoyed and even angry at each other. Over time, the issue is no longer about personality differences but the character of their spouse. "He cares more about his spreadsheets than me!" "She has zero discipline when it concerns our money!" Are personality differences and irritation an indicator of spiritual warfare? Not necessarily. However, applying our principle, harboring ill feelings and simmering anger toward each other *is* an indicator Satan is actively seeking to establish a foothold in your marriage. Continuing to allow ill feelings or impatience with each other to take root is allowing Satan to make the most of the opportunity handed to him by pulling you deeper along the continuum toward the flesh. In short, Ken and Maria's irritation toward each other as they make the hard transition into marriage may not constitute spiritual attack. However, allowing deeds of the flesh to fester in the midst of the transition most *certainly* provides the devil the opportunity to establish a foothold and should be treated as such.

In addition to our broad principle, are there other specific indicators that spiritual battle is at play? In researching this topic I read dozens of books from Christian authors, theologians, and philosophers—past and present—that focus on spiritual warfare. Each addressed the issue of diagnosing the demonic. While authors disagree at times, there are certain signs that make everyone's list. Before I present the five most common symptoms of demonic activity, it would be wise to address a thorny question: Can Satan plant thoughts in the minds of believers? This issue is pertinent because most of the symptoms I'll explore focus on our thoughts.

CAN SATAN INFLUENCE OUR THOUGHTS?

Theologian Keith Ferdinando, after studying the reality of spiritual warfare in both the Old and New Testaments, concludes, "A critical theatre of the believer's spiritual warfare is the battle for the mind."[4] Christian author Kenneth Boa concurs and states that spiritual attacks are predominantly "characterized by obsessive thoughts and behavior."[5]

The Scriptures give several examples of Satan's ability to put thoughts into our minds. In the Old Testament we learn that "Satan rose up against Israel and incited David to take a census of Israel" (1 Chron 21:1). While it may seem wise for a king to know the size and strength of his troops, we later learn David had slowly shifted his confidence from the Lord to his military strength. Though warned by his advisers, David insisted the census be taken, resulting in a stunning defeat for Israel. In the New Testament we see Satan is able to put the idea of betrayal into the heart of Judas (Jn 13:2) and greed into the mind of Ananias to lie about the amount of an offering to the church (Acts 5:3). Even Jesus experienced Satan's ability to plant thoughts. During his wilderness tempting, Satan takes Jesus up to the top of a mountain and shows him the splendor of all earthly kingdoms. Theologians note that from that small mountain it would be impossible for Jesus to see the kingdoms of the world. Therefore, Satan must have had the ability to project into Jesus's mind a panoramic picture of these kingdoms.[6]

The German theologian Martin Luther offers one of the most vivid accounts of a Christian coming to terms with a battle for his mind. He writes, "The Devil throws hideous thoughts in the soul— hatred of God, blasphemy, and despair. . . . He disputes with me and makes me give birth to all kinds of strange thoughts."[7] In the following section we'll consider some of the "strange thoughts" Satan encourages spouses to adopt toward each other, themselves, and even God.

TOP FIVE INDICATORS OF SPIRITUAL WARFARE

What are the signs or symptoms of the demonic most theologians and authors take note of? While St. Ignatius's rule can give Maria and Ken—and the rest of us—a general idea if spiritual opposition is occurring, the following signs can add clarity.

Inappropriate anger. In instructing us about anger, the apostle Paul makes an interesting observation. "In your anger do not sin" (Eph 4:26). He wisely notes that anger in and of itself is not necessarily sin. In fact, there are times when anger is the appropriate response. This is good news for those of us who are married. In the course of doing life together, disagreements—and even anger—are part and parcel of marriage. At marriage conferences I speak at, I often have couples turn to each other and say, "We argue too!" However, Paul is quick to warn that anger can easily open the door for sin. The Scriptures state that we should be careful our anger does not lead to evil (Ps 37:8), which is why only the foolish give "full vent to their rage" (Prov 29:11). Kay, a friend of mine, finds it helpful to think of anger as you would the layout of a house. To her, anger is like the foyer of a house. "The foyer is not a room you are supposed to stay in, decorate, or camp out. It is meant to move us into the house." While anger may be helpful in motivating us to address interpersonal conflict, we should not camp out there and let it build.[8]

One of the central problems with chronic anger is that it profoundly colors our perspective of another person. Most of us understand that no person is all good or all bad. However, an angry person can easily lose sight of the good a spouse does and only focus on the bad. "Do not be quickly provoked in your spirit," admonishes Solomon (Eccles 7:9). A habitually angry person is *always* provoked by the actions of a spouse. Anger, if unchecked, can lead to bitterness, which communication theorists define as *anger that has cemented.* If you find yourself stuck in a rut where everything your spouse does makes you angry, then it would be wise to consider, as Paul does, how your anger may have given the devil a foothold (Eph 4:26).

In some cases, unchecked anger can explode into violence. Tragically, battery is the single largest cause of injury to women—more frequent than auto accidents, muggings, and rapes combined.[9] If violence of any kind is present in a marriage or relationship, not only should demonic opposition be suspected, but the battered spouse should immediately seek safety, protection, and professional help.

Physical abuse—hitting, hair pulling, shoving—is not the only form of abuse. *Verbal abuse* consists of words intended to shame, demean, or threaten another person. The book of Proverbs powerfully states that the tongue "crushes the spirit" (Prov 15:4). *Emotional abuse* is nonphysical behavior designed to control, isolate, punish, or berate a person. Emotional abuse can also entail destroying or purposefully misplacing objects that have great personal value to the abused, such as cherished family photos or gifts made by children.

Sense of impending doom. Due to financial pressures, potential parenting issues, disagreements, and unexpected health issues, all marriages go through anxiety-producing stretches. What if one of our jobs gets axed? Are we saving enough? Are the kids making the right kinds of friends? Will we ever be able to have children? What if my health deteriorates *more*? When faced with anxiety, followers of Christ are to respond with prayer and thanksgiving, resulting in a peace from God that "transcends all understanding" and stands guard over our hearts and minds (Phil 4:6-7).

But what if you simply cannot shake a deep-rooted sense of dread? Will our most recent argument irrevocably rupture the marriage? If we take this financial step of faith, will we be ruined? If I put my foot down with the kids, will they hate me? Our sense of hopefulness is replaced with deep resignation that people or situations are only going to get worse.

Violent dreams. You wake up with your heart pounding! Images of your spouse dying or children being separated from you during a violent accident seemed so *real*. The all-encompassing *fear* you felt is hard to shake. You lie back down with eyes wide open, staring at the ceiling. One of my colleagues taught a class on spiritual battle for years and told me that over one-third of his students consistently reported disturbing dreams that they suspected had demonic origins. Why? In his groundbreaking study of the human psyche, psychologist Abraham Maslow argued our most primal need as humans is safety. In violent dreams, however, we feel profoundly unsafe. Such fear not only saps our sleep but makes us approach the day with apprehension—what if the dream comes true? How safe am I?

No longer believing the best about God. In his letter to believers in Rome, Paul asks a poignant question: "If God is for us, who can be against us?" (Rom 8:31). His point is, based on all he had written previously in his letter, believers should be utterly convinced that nothing is able to "separate us from the love of God that is in Christ Jesus our Lord" (v. 39). However, many Christians, and even biblical writers, report feelings of being abandoned by God. One psalmist accuses God of being asleep as the armies of Israel are soundly defeated. His conclusion: "Surely in vain I have kept my heart pure" (Ps 73:13). When a spouse struggling in a marriage no longer feels God is on their side or, even worse, asleep at the wheel as a marriage struggles, it is a strong indicator of demonic activity.

An interesting twist to this symptom is that when a spouse is struggling to believe that God is still on their side, Satan plants the thought that such doubt is so unbecoming of a true child of God that going back to him is no longer possible. In essence, a spiritual line has been crossed and the person is no longer welcome by God. Such thoughts are indicators the devil is trying to shame a believer into permanent separation from the heavenly Father.

No longer believing the best about you. Psychologists tell us that the most important part of who we are is our self-talk—the internal dialogue we continually have with ourselves. Our self-talk centers around three fundamental questions: How do I look *in* comparison to others? How do I do *in* comparison to others? How important am I *in* comparison to others? In today's body-image world of thin and often medically altered people, how do I physically measure up? In a social world where we are often judged by our bank accounts or status, how do I stack up to fellow coworkers or friends? Am I important to anyone?

As Christian couples, we are called to continually put the needs of our spouses above our own. Yet, when we evaluate ourselves via self-talk, how well do we think we are doing? Here is where Satan seeks to influence our internal conversation. As biblical writers studied Satan, they assigned him certain names, such as liar (Jn 8:44) and accuser (Rev 12:10). Satan seeks to influence our self-talk by accusing us of abysmally falling short of biblical standards. For example, all couples struggle with balancing the demands of work with the needs of our spouse. Sometimes work takes a priority over our spouse or family. What is the difference between a healthy assessment of priorities and spiritual attack?

At this point, we must make a crucial distinction between guilt (I should make my spouse a priority) and the shaming tactics of Satan (I'm a terrible person). Christian author and psychologist Curt Thompson helps distinguish between the two. "Guilt is something I feel because I have done something bad. Shame is something I feel because I *am* bad."[10] Thompson notes one of the destructive consequences of feeling shame is that it isolates us from those we love in that "shame separates us from others, as my awareness of what I feel is virtually consumed with my own internal sensations."[11] A similar thought was expressed by German theologian and political activist Dietrich Bonhoeffer, who observed, "The more isolated a person is, the more destructive will be the power of sin over him, and the more deeply he becomes involved in it, the more disastrous the isolation."[12]

To summarize, while guilt can be an appropriate response to behavior and even prompted by the conviction of the Holy Spirit

(2 Cor 7:9-10), shame is never from God. While we may at times fall short of wedding vows or biblical commands, we remain deeply loved and accepted by God as his children (1 Jn 3:1).

 While not appearing on all lists, what were other signs of the demonic noted by scholars? An honorable mention list would include the following: strong aversion to the name of Jesus, inability to renounce a dominating sin, inability to pray, difficulty making connections with fellow Christians, personal or family problems that do not respond to therapy, physical problems that do not respond to medication, and sins that are resistant to spiritual disciplines such as fasting or prayer.

SPECIAL CONSIDERATION: SEXUAL INTIMACY

While the previous list is helpful, my experience speaking at marriage conferences prompts me to add another sign of possible demonic activity—a warped view of sexual intimacy. Being tempted to view sex in unhealthy ways is strong evidence of demonic influence and temptation.

First, our view of sex becomes warped when we elevate it over other equally valuable forms of love. Before we married, I was a hopeless romantic who was deeply impressed by the idea of passionate love. As a theater major in college I was constantly exposed to grandiose ideas of love played out larger than life on a magnificent stage. It's not that passionate love doesn't have a place in marriage, but it is often shortsighted of other kinds of love. Erotic or passionate love that characterizes the first stages of a relationship will undoubtedly fluctuate in intensity throughout the life of the marriage. Satan delights in tempting married couples to judge their intimacy exclusively on one type of love.

When the ancient Greeks wanted to describe the many forms of love, they used a wide array of terms such as *ludus* (playful love), *pragma* (pragmatic love), and *agape* (divine love). Their two favorite terms were *eros* and *storge*. Eros is powerful romantic love that flares up quickly and expresses itself in dramatic ways. Storge, or the love between friends, is slow to develop but durable.

Erotic lovers experience all the soaring peaks and gut-wrenching plunges of an emotional rollercoaster: euphoria, happiness, calm, panic, despair. They are adrenaline junkies who desperately seek to experience new thrills. The problem, as any married couple will readily admit, is that love and commitment are often expressed through mundane, daily responsibilities and sacrifices more associated with friends than lovers. Individuals I've met who have had an emotional or physical affair often confess a yearning for a return of the thrills of erotic love. Over time, the commitments of marriage slowly suffocated the passion of the marriage. Satan delights in stoking the desire for a return to the early stages of romance.

The Scriptures seem to suggest that passion, romance, and friendship are bound up together. It's not that passion should dissipate as the marriage matures, but rather passion is stoked by other forms of love. Solomon's bride states that her lover is radiant and compares his body to "polished ivory" (Song 5:14). She's not embarrassed to admit that when she feels his touch her heart pounds (v. 4). What stirs such powerful romantic feelings? After sensually describing her husband's body she states, "This is my beloved, this is *my friend*, daughters of Jerusalem" (v. 16, emphasis added). Her friendship with and romantic feelings for Solomon were inseparable.[13]

Like Solomon's bride, Noreen and I have discovered that our passion is fueled the more we work on our friendship. As the commitments of work, church, and family grow, we need to make time for us to engage in activities we *both* enjoy. No matter how busy our week is, we reserve Wednesdays to attend a yoga class together. Often, we have to suppress laughter as we try to do seemingly impossible stances or positions. After the class, we stop to get coffee and talk. We find that these times of connection not only produce playful friendship love (*ludus/storge*) but also passion (*eros*). Most importantly, it also builds our spiritual defenses against Satan's attempt to judge our marriage merely on one isolated form of love.

Second, our view of sex becomes warped when we allow unrighteous views to color our perspective. Culture watcher Naomi Wolf argues that today's influx of pornography via technology is having two devastating effects on how we view sex and romantic love. First, she notes that men and women take their cues from porn and "are indeed being taught what sex is, how it looks, what its etiquette and expectations are, by pornographic training—and this is having a huge effect on how they interact."[14] As I write this, *Fifty Shades Freed*—the third installment of the *Fifty Shades of Grey* franchise—opened the weekend before Valentine's Day and was the top grossing film for that day. Its ability to romanticize physical abuse was not limited to American audiences as it pulled in 97 million dollars in worldwide sales.[15]

As women increasingly consume porn they realize that they—with all their imperfections—simply cannot compete with vivid fantasies internalized by boyfriends and husbands. They worry "that as mere flesh and blood, they can scarcely get, let alone hold, their attention." Wolf concludes by offering this chilling assessment: "Today, real naked women are just bad porn."[16]

Long before today's porn saturation, King Solomon gives an alternative view of sexual excitement. Looking at his young wife, he comments her legs are "like jewels, the work of an artist's hands" (Song 7:1) and her breasts are "like two fawns, like twin fawns of a gazelle" (v. 3). Not only is the king "captivated" by his wife's natural beauty, but he affirms, "how beautiful you are and how pleasing" (v. 6). In altering today's cultural terrain, Satan delights in making natural beauty seem boring and void of *eros*. The result is a sex life that seems lacking and unexciting. For couples intent on resisting today's pornification of desire, our level of sexual intimacy and pleasure can be an indicator of not only the overall health of the marriage but whether demonic tempting is occurring.

KEN AND MARIA REVISITED

With this new information, Ken and Maria are now better equipped to diagnose the potential of spiritual opposition. While all couples experience irritation or anger toward each other, is Ken's anger toward Maria becoming chronic and coloring his view of *all* of her good qualities? Are Maria's thoughts toward Ken spiraling downward, producing deeper levels of anger? As a couple are they increasingly starting to think the marriage may not make it if they keep getting irritated with each other? Has this irritation even spilled over into their view of God? After all, wasn't it God who led them together in the first place? As they struggle transitioning into marriage, their spiritual antenna should alert them that no longer believing the best about their spouse or themselves could be a sign of spiritual battle. Like Ken and Maria, if we suspect spiritual opposition is at play, our response should be comprehensive. The signs of demonic activity we've been considering should not be considered in isolation from physical, relational, or psychological problems. The follower of Christ should utilize a wide-ranging approach to anxiety, fear, or marital struggles that entails consulting doctors, marital counselors, psychologists, and spiritual advisers.

READER	Excuse me.
AUTHOR	You're back.
READER	I told you I might have more questions.
AUTHOR	Okay, what's on your mind?
READER	I get that demons can influence what I think, or do, but how *much* influence?
AUTHOR	Are you asking if, as a child of God, you can be possessed?
READER	Yes! I'll be honest, even the possibility is unnerving!
AUTHOR	When theologians talk about varying degrees of demonic activity, they usually break it down into influence, oppression, and demonization. *Influence* includes what we've discussed in this chapter—the ability to plant thoughts into our minds or manipulate our self-talk. *Oppression* is when a clear foothold has been allowed to exist in the life of a believer, such as refusing to forgive a person or allowing anger to build unchecked.

READER   Got it. What about demonization like we see in the movies where a person's eyes roll back and she speaks in guttural Latin phrases? As a Christian, am I susceptible to such a hostile takeover?

AUTHOR   This is a debated topic, but most theologians agree that while demons can exert significant influence, they cannot penetrate the core of a believer and take away what God has given (such as forgiveness, redemption, salvation, adoption into God's family, and the Holy Spirit). The fact that the Holy Spirit indwells believers (Jn 14:17; Rom 8:9; 1 Cor 6:19-20) makes it impossible for a demonic entity to also indwell and assume full control of a believer. Simply put, demons do not have the ability to kick out or evict the Holy Spirit in the life of a believer.[17] Does that ease your anxiety?

READER   A little. Thanks.

While these principles for diagnosing spiritual opposition are helpful, what should we do if we are still undecided whether or not evil forces are at play? Military history teaches us that there is danger in *underestimating* an enemy. During the Battle of Britain, both the Germans and British made key *mis*calculations about each other's strength. The misunderstanding centered on how to calculate a fighter squadron. To the Germans, a squadron consisted of twelve airplanes, while the British considered a squadron to be twenty planes. When the Germans learned of the number of fighter squadrons the British had, they multiplied it by twelve planes and were encouraged by the low numbers. Conversely, the British over-estimated the strength of their enemy by assuming each German squadron had eight more planes than it actually did.

While both sides were mistaken, their mistakes were not equal. War strategists note that if you are going to err, it is better to *over-estimate* the enemy's strength. Thinking that the German air force was greater in number, the British took steps to meet the strong threat. However, the Germans let down their guard and thought victory would come easily. "Give me four sunny days and I'll crush the Royale Air Force," a key German commander famously bragged. In the end, Hitler's miscalculation proved costly.

When it comes to spiritual battle and our marriages, how should we view the strength and activity of the evil one? Is it better to err in overestimating demonic activity rather than underestimating? As American Christians, have we—for fear of overreacting or looking foolish—consistently underestimated the strength of Satan? As a result, have we lowered our defenses to spiritual opposition?

In the Scriptures, writers have no qualms about assessing the strength of the evil one. Mark describes Satan as a "strong man" due to widespread authority (Mk 3:27). John informs us that this authority and influence extends across our entire planet (1 Jn 5:19). Peter graphically reminds us that the evil one is on the prowl looking for victims (1 Pet 5:8). Taking our cue from Scripture, if there is any suspicion that spiritual opposition is occurring, a couple should treat that threat as being real and act appropriately.

INTERVIEW: SIGNS OF SPIRITUAL INFLUENCE

Chris Grace has been a professor of psychology for almost thirty years and serves as the director of Biola's Center for Marriage and Relationships. His entire professional career has been spent studying human behavior. Over the years, he's seen it all.

TIM   As you think through your career, what are some of
           your most interesting challenges?

CHRIS   I did an internship with the criminally insane and
           then worked as a counselor in a home that housed
           up to fifty adolescent boys—ranging in age from
           twelve to eighteen years old—who had behavioral
           problems. Later my wife and I supervised a home for
           runaway teens in Orange County, California. In
           those settings we often worked with very troubled
           people and their families.

TIM   What were the challenges?

CHRIS   Many struggle with regulating emotions, problems
           in relationships, confused thinking, and anger issues
           that often resulted in harm being done to themselves
           or others. As a Christian, I viewed situations and our
           interactions through a scientific and psychological
           lens, as well as spiritual. Over time, I started to notice
           indicators that some type of evil influence perhaps
           was at play. Some signs caught my attention from a
           spiritual perspective, especially with those who were
           most disturbed.

TIM   Can you briefly describe them?

CHRIS   Sure. For some there was a strong negative reaction
           to the name of Jesus. In most cases when I asked if I
           could pray for a person, they would be totally open
           or even appreciative. However, a few would get agi-
           tated and even angry when we started to pray using
           Jesus' name. That makes sense since the Scriptures

tell us that not only do demons recognize God but they shudder at his name (Jas 2:19).

TIM   What's next?

CHRIS   Second, especially with those struggling with psychotic disorders, there would be confused thoughts or speech—called a *word salad*.

TIM   Can you give an example?

CHRIS   A person struggling with a mental disorder may believe people are out to get them or are watching and following them, and they may speak in a mixed-up jumble of words and phrases that don't make much sense or are overtly paranoid. In contrast, a person dealing with potential demonic influences may actually have more logical, clear reasoning and thoughts. The next one is a little unsettling.

TIM   You have my attention.

CHRIS   On rare occasions, people may have access to what I'd call supernatural information. For example, a small group of people, one who was a friend of mine, once confronted and began to pray with a person they suspected was demonically influenced. When one person in the group mentioned the name of Jesus, the person being confronted quickly responded, "Who are you to use that name [Jesus]? Why don't you tell your friends what's under your bed?" It turns out that the man doing the confronting had a deep pornography addiction that included hiding magazines and videos under his bed. He had kept this addiction hidden from everyone. Or so he thought.

TIM   So, you think this information came to this person via a demon?

CHRIS   It seems a possibility. If demons observe us, then they may be privy to deeds we think are hidden from others.

TIM   That gives me chills. Let's move on.

CHRIS   Last, I would say that for a lot of people with psychological issues, psychotropic medications such as antidepressants often work well enough over time to decrease symptoms like confused or paranoid thinking. Such medications will not, however, have much of an impact on the speech or behavior of a person who is dealing with demonic spiritual influence.

TIM   These have been helpful. Thanks.

CHRIS   As a Christian psychologist I want to make sure I'm open to both psychological and spiritual indicators. We should never rush into a quick diagnosis in either direction or prematurely rule out certain causes if signs persist.

TIM   In addition to being a professor of psychology, you also give direction to a center focusing on marriage and relationships. What are some indicators—while not as dramatic as what you've just mentioned—that a couple may be facing spiritual opposition?

CHRIS   Sure. I believe that most marital problems—mine included—come from poor communication patterns or unhealthy ways of dealing with conflict. However, my spiritual antenna goes up when couples move from struggling with something to being consumed by it. For example, all of us struggle from time to time with forgiving a spouse. However, there is a big difference between struggling to forgive and allowing bitterness or hard-heartedness to take root and dominate our thoughts. The bitterness opens a door for negative spiritual influence.

TIM The bitterness makes the couple vulnerable.

CHRIS Yes. And it's not merely bitterness or lack of forgiveness that can make us vulnerable. Greed can also make us susceptible. If I start to love money or status more than God, then a void has been created. As we well know, a void can easily be filled with other things. As my love for money *increases*, my love for God *decreases*. All the while, Satan keeps whispering in my ear to pursue more—*more* status, *more* power, *more* likes, *more* money.

TIM How can a couple respond to this whispering?

CHRIS Make sure to keep your heart open to God. You may not be ready to fully forgive your spouse, but keep your heart open to God's command to forgive and remember how much he has forgiven you. Staying open to God during our marital struggles ensures that there is not room for Satan to gain traction.

TIM Drown out Satan's whispering with God's voice via the Holy Spirit or the Scriptures.

CHRIS Exactly.

CONTINUING THE CONVERSATION

1. While no relationship is perfect, do Paul's descriptors of the flesh outnumber the qualities of the Spirit in your marriage? What deed of the flesh most pulls you in? Conversely, what fruit of the Spirit is most characteristic of your marriage?

2. What is your reaction to the possibility that demonic forces may be influencing your specific thoughts? Of the top indicators of spiritual oppression—inappropriate anger, impending doom, violent dreams, not believing the best about God or yourself, a warped view of sexuality—which most applies to you individually? Which do you suspect applies to your spouse?

3. If sexual intimacy is an indicator of the overall health of your relationship, how then would you describe your current level of sexual intimacy? How free do you feel to discuss sexual issues with each other?

4. In your marriage, how much is the possibility of spiritual oppression or influence on your radar as a couple? Why or why not?

4

THE SERPENT WAS CRAFTY

UNDERSTANDING
THE TACTICS OF SATAN

*W*hat's the one thing all successful generals have in common?

Military historian and former combat commander Bevin Alexander spent a lifetime answering this question. Is it superior force, advanced weaponry, or a new type of psychological warfare? Alexander suggests that successful generals seldom deviate from one fundamental tactic: attack from behind. He writes, "Great generals realize that a rear attack distracts, dislocates, and often defeats an enemy physically by cutting him off from his supplies and reinforcements."[1] The result? The enemy is mentally undermined and a sense of security dashed.

Do Alexander's observations of great generals equally apply to Satan? In tempting Adam and Eve, did he mount a frontal assault or deceptively attack from the rear? Why was his strategy successful? What caused the first humans to succumb to his maneuvers?

In this chapter we will take a behind the scenes look at Satan's strategy for tempting Adam and Eve in the unique surroundings of paradise, and then transition to how he might undermine our marriages in a modern setting.

THE FIRST TEMPTING

Imagine the world Adam and Eve inhabited. An ecosystem free of pollution and decay that God himself deems "very good" (Gen 1:31). The crowning creative act is to form two humans who reflect God's image (v. 27). Adam and Eve experience a sense of interpersonal intimacy—void of shame—which is poetically described as "one flesh" (Gen 2:24). This intimacy is not limited to each other but also extends to their Creator. In the cool of the day, God regularly strolls through paradise to interact with all he has created—especially Adam and Eve. The first two chapters of Genesis give no warning that an encounter is about to happen that will not only rupture the shalom of paradise but also have dire consequences for our future world and marriages.

One day, a serpent approaches Eve. As we read the Genesis narrative our spiritual defenses immediately go up! "Eve, be careful!" Yet, it is important to note that in a pre-fall world there was no reason for Eve to be suspicious. For modern readers, a snake or serpent is seen as shifty and repulsive, but to Eve it was just another creature. "Satan was careful not to appear in a form that would terrorize her or arouse revulsion," notes J. Oswald Sanders. To do so would only "throw her back into the arms of God. Instead, he chose as his instrument an attractive but inferior animal."[2] In the Genesis narrative, the serpent is described as being more "crafty" than all the other beasts.

The Hebrew word for "crafty" can also be translated as "prudent," which, in the book of Proverbs, carries a positive connotation (Prov 12:16; 14:8; 22:3; 27:12). To be prudent is to be wise, careful, and discrete. However, the serpent uses his careful observations about paradise, humans, and God not only to understand but to undermine Eve. While the Genesis text never specifically identifies the serpent as Satan, New Testament writers such as John inform us that the "ancient serpent" was in fact Satan (Rev 20:2).

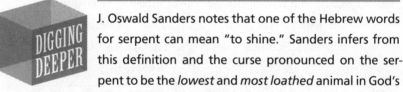

J. Oswald Sanders notes that one of the Hebrew words for serpent can mean "to shine." Sanders infers from this definition and the curse pronounced on the serpent to be the *lowest* and *most loathed* animal in God's creation (Gen 3:14) that before the curse he was characterized by splendor and beauty. Thus, originally this shining creature would have not awakened in Eve suspicion but rather curiosity. Tragically, what God had made in splendor was twisted by Satan into worldwide revulsion.

As we read the Genesis narrative there is little sense of urgency in Satan's conversation with Eve. He is not presented as nervously looking around or being pushy, but rather having a long, calculating conversation with Eve. If we can assume that it took Adam a significant amount of time to study and name the entire animal kingdom—though it is described in a mere two verses (Gen 2:19-20)—can we not also assume that the serpent's successful tempting of Eve lasted longer than a condensed six verse description offered by the biblical writer (Gen 3:1-6)? When reading the Genesis account, it is important to keep in mind that we are not reading a transcript of the conversation between Eve and the serpent, but rather the bullet points of what occurred. Thus, we can assume it took long periods of time for Eve—at the serpent's prompting—to grow increasingly distrustful of her Creator, resulting in rebellion.

Christian writer D. G. Kehl gives us a sense of the slow progression sin takes: "We do not fall in a moment." Rather, the "predisposition to yield to sin has been forming, building, germinating—but not necessarily consciously so." Kehl chillingly concludes that Satan "plants subtle stimuli, often subliminal ones; he influences an attitude; he wins a 'minor' victory—always in preparation for the 'big fall.'"[3]

DIGGING DEEPER

How long did Eve's temptation take? In his space trilogy's second novel, *Perelandra*, C. S. Lewis paints the picture of a planet that resembles earth but has not been touched by sin. In this pristine world we meet a character simply described as the Green Lady, who is this planet's version of Eve. Her tempter is not a snake but a sinister scientist named Weston, who is determined to cause the Green Lady's downfall. The Green Lady engages in deep conversations with Weston that span days in which she is challenged spiritually, emotionally, and intellectually. Through the narrator, Ransom, we learn that the Green Lady's tempter relentlessly presses in on her with sophisticated arguments that produce an "enchantment" that seems to deepen "in her mind every moment." In a chilling observation, the narrator states that Weston's arguments were "always very nearly true."*

---

*C. S. Lewis, *Perelandra* (New York: Collier, 1965), 135.

THE SERPENT'S TACTICS

As we read the biblical text, we see Kehl's observation played out as the serpent not only creates in Eve a predisposition to sin but wins minor victories that ultimately lead to a tragic fall.

Tactic 1. Suggestion rather than argument. The serpent begins his conversation with Eve with a suggestion rather than an argument. In other words, the serpent didn't begin with, "Eve, God is just plain wrong," but rather, "Did God really say?" (Gen 3:1). Asserting that God is wrong would amount to a frontal attack, while suggesting that his command is open to interpretation is an attack from the rear. Offering a suggestion, rather than an argument not only keeps Eve's defenses down but "smuggles in the assumption that God's word is subject to our judgment."[4]

In this first tactic, the serpent is not concerned with the exact wording of God's command but subtly questions God's authority to issue such commands. After all, God has given Eve enormous freedom in how she operates in paradise. Who is to say God's authority will *always* trump her free will? Depending on the situation, is it possible that Eve's point of view can be on par with God's opinion? That's the conclusion many young Americans have reached today concerning the moral authority of the Bible. According to a massive survey conducted by the Barna Research Group in conjunction with InterVarsity Christian Fellowship and the American Bible Society, nearly half (45 percent) of young unchurched adults in America view the Bible as "an instructional book of stories and advice compiled by men."[5] In other words, biblical stories are merely one perspective among the myriads of stories or advice in culture. This first tactic came at Eve in the form of two questions: Did God really say? And if he did, so what?

Tactic 2. Present the Creator as restrictive and insecure. In the
Genesis narrative we observe the serpent twisting God's words in
order to present him as being overly restrictive and stingy.

The serpent asks a seemingly simple question: "Did God really
say, 'You must not eat from any tree in the garden?'" (Gen 3:1).
From the serpent's perspective, how odd that God would place Eve
in paradise but then tell her she can only look but not touch. In
Wendell Berry's poem "The Peace of Wild Things," people live in a
society that produces despair and anxiety.[6] Berry's remedy is to lay
down in deep pine woods and take in the beauty of nature to observe how peacefully the wood drake lies on the water and how
the trees and stars offer grace and freedom. In paradise, Adam and
Eve live out what Berry suggests. The first couple were free of
anxiety, inhabiting an ecosystem that they were to not only care for
but enjoy. Can you imagine God telling them they could not fully
partake of magnificent fruit hanging from ubiquitous trees? We
cannot because God *never* placed that restriction on them. Cor-
recting the serpent, Eve properly responds that no tree or fruit is
off-limits *except* the tree of the knowledge of good and evil that
occupies the center of the garden (Gen 3:3).

Caught in his distortion, the serpent shifts to the qualities of
the restricted tree. We read the tree was "good for food," "pleasing
to the eye," and most importantly, "desirable for gaining wisdom"
(Gen 3:6). If the tree offered so much, why would God make it off-
limits? The serpent suggests that in eating the fruit, Eve's eyes
would be opened and she would be like God in her understanding
of right and wrong (Gen 3:4). Why wouldn't God want Eve to have
deeper moral understanding?

There are two misconceptions about the tree of the knowledge of good and evil. First, eating of the tree would give Adam and Eve a godlike knowledge of both. Not so. The phrase *knowledge of good and evil* is a Near Eastern literary device that only suggests a deeper level of moral reasoning, not exhaustive knowledge. Second, we mistakenly assume the tree was permanently off-limits. From God's perspective the issue was not *should* Adam and Eve gain deeper moral reasoning but *when*. There is nothing wrong with the desire to cook over an open fire; it just isn't for toddlers. The central question surrounding the forbidden tree was: Who was in the best position to judge if Adam and Eve were ready to handle this complex form of moral reasoning? Would the first humans submit to God's timetable for deeper moral knowledge or speed up the process?[7]

Slowly, Eve began to buy into the serpent's depiction of the Creator as restrictive (all fruit is off-limits), insecure (a human will not become like the Creator), and unreasonable (fruit good to the eyes should be enjoyed).

Tactic 3. Minimize the outcome of rebellion. As Eve's thinking becomes more muddled, she snaps back to reality by remembering what God told her would be the consequence of disobedience: "You will die" (Gen 3:3). The serpent confidently counters, "You surely will not die" (v. 4). Modern translation: God is being overly dramatic. The consequences of going your own way will not be nearly as bad as advertised. Minimizing the effects of ignoring God's commands is a time-honored tactic relevant to today.

- Yes, leaving my spouse for another will cause short-term pain. However, starting a new life with this person is worth it, and in the end the kids will come around when they see how happy I am.

- Looking at porn is fine so long as I control it. It's not like I'm cheating on my spouse; it's just images. Besides, no one needs to know.

- Sure, God commands me to forgive. But not with *this* person. I will not be walked on in this marriage. When my spouse gets his act together, then I'll forgive.

- There's nothing wrong with a little flirting with an old friend over Facebook. Really, we are just reconnecting and catching up. I must admit, it is nice to have someone appreciate me. I'm tired of my spouse ignoring me.

To modern hearers, Satan subtly suggests, "Are extramarital affairs, pornography, harboring bitterness, and breaking emotional boundaries really the end of the world?"

Tactic 4. Divide and conquer. Perhaps the four most puzzling words in the Genesis narrative are "who was with her" (Gen 3:6). As we have considered Eve's interaction with the serpent, you may have wondered, *Where was Adam?* The text surprisingly states that when Eve finally succumbs to temptation, evidenced by eating the forbidden fruit, she "also gave some to her husband, who was with her, and he ate it" (Gen 3:6). Old Testament scholar John Walton notes that all the verbs in this narrative are plural. "From verse one where the serpent addresses the woman but uses the plural 'you,' to the woman's use of inclusionary 'we' and the serpent's description of the results formulated to both, there is grammatical indication that both were there."[8]

If we grant that Adam was physically there, a larger question surfaces: How was the serpent able to psychologically isolate the two from each other? In this narrative we witness Satan's most effective strategic principle: couples do not need to be physically separate to be isolated from each other.

In the hurriedness of life, we have all experienced this reality. As couples, we race to meet daily responsibilities—shuffling kids to activities, caring for aging parents, working extra hours to make ends meet—which over time takes a toll on our relational intimacy. With decreased levels of intimacy, we at best become roommates, and at worst, strangers. The indie rock band Death Cab for Cutie describes the isolation that can happen even when sharing a bed. In their haunting song "Brothers on a Hotel Bed," we meet a couple who unexpectedly falls in love and eventually marry. At first, they take endless motorbike rides. She is the passenger, arms outstretched pretending to take flight. Yet over time they grow isolated and distant. After a quick "Goodnight," they sleep on separate sides of the mattress like brothers forced to share a hotel bed; making sure not to touch. Can you relate? After speaking at marriage conferences for over twenty years, I've heard from countless couples that their most common complaint is loneliness.

While it is interesting to observe the serpent interact with our ancestors, how is this relevant to my marriage? Rather than living in paradise, we live in a modest house struggling to pay down the mortgage, put a little away for retirement each month, and try to be responsible parents. How do the devil's strategies apply today?

FROM PARADISE TO YOUR MARRIAGE

In a letter to a young, struggling church in Corinth, the apostle Paul not only notes that "Eve was deceived by the serpent's cunning," but that the *Corinthians'* minds may also be "led astray" (2 Cor 11:3). In other words, Satan did not stop with Adam and Eve. He has been perfecting his technique by tempting Christians in every generation. How might he take the tactics he learned in the garden and honed throughout centuries and go after your marriage?

James and Jen: A test case. Married with two kids, James and Jen manage an often hectic life. Both former high school athletes, they are interested in getting their two daughters into sports. Their oldest, Kendra (13), has been recruited by a youth travel volleyball club. While both are intrigued by this invitation, Jen is increasingly hesitant when they learn committing entails traveling most weekends and a significant financial investment. James thinks it is a great opportunity and they should go for it, while Jen wonders about how it will affect their family and an already tight budget. Having witnessed the serpent in action in the Garden, how might he subtlety approach this couple?

Early stages of conflict. Long before this particular conflict, Satan had already been at work in James and Jen individually. As we have already noted, Satan desires to "influence an attitude" in order to win "minor" victories in hopes of securing a "big fall."

Through the normal struggles in a marriage, James and Jen have periodically struggled to believe the best about each other. While James appreciates Jen's desire to put money away for the future, he can easily see it as being stingy. Conversely, Jen admires James's desire to be involved with the girls' athletics, but she sometimes wonders if it is more about him and his desire to be the parent of sought-after athletes. Over time, it becomes easy to see each other in a negative light. Jen views her husband as envious of other parents on the select volleyball team, while James begins to attribute selfishness toward his wife, who seemingly cares more about the bank account than developing a gifted child. Compounding the issue is that, due to hectic schedules, they have had no time to fully discuss these valid concerns. Rather, they slowly start to let ill feelings toward each other take root.

Unexpressed feelings such as the ones experienced by James and Jen are identified as *latent conflict* because anger and disappointment simmer *below* the surface. To use the apostle Paul's language, a spiritual foothold has been allowed to form by not dealing with concerns head-on and in a timely manner. Like Adam and Eve, James and Jen have allowed the devil to ever-so-slowly isolate each from one another. This latent conflict will complicate discussing their daughter's possible involvement with a travel team.

Middle stages of conflict. As the deadline for registration approaches, a sense of urgency engulfs the couple. Seeking to exploit Jen's legitimate concerns about the cost of a traveling team, Satan seeks to foster a sense of impending doom. Jen wrestles with growing anxiety: *What if Jenni [11] also wants to play on a team? There is no way we can afford two player fees! Do we say yes to one and no to the other? What about church? Is it something we do only when there isn't a tournament? Does James not care about their spiritual welfare?* Similarly, James is increasingly convinced his daughter is good enough to play at the college level, and his wife—rather than being excited—is choosing to be a roadblock. His anxiety is spurred by one powerful thought: *This opportunity may never come again!* Interpersonal conflict is fueled when participants start to perceive incompatible goals (financial security versus stewarding athletic gifts) and a battle for limited resources (fixed income and limited time).

Finally, James and Jen sit down to hash it out. The registration deadline is in one week and a decision has to be made. The problem is, due to harboring ill feelings toward each other, the couple will most likely experience a harsh start-up to the conversation. The first three minutes of a disagreement is the most important because it establishes the relational level (amount of love, respect, and compassion between individuals) of the entire conversation.

When the discussion starts, James and Jen exhibit poor listening by engaging in *cross-complaining*, which occurs when one person's complaint is met by a counter complaint. "James, you're letting your dream of seeing our girls play on a travel team blind you to the significant costs of being on that team," Jen asserts. "Well, all you see is the bottom line of our bank account," James shoots back. As the discussion heats up, each adopts an increasingly negative view of the other. As the negativity builds, interruptions become more common, voices are raised, and feelings are hurt. While each is aware of Paul's admonition to speak truth in love (Eph 4:15), each finds it increasingly difficult to present their views in a loving manner.

Later stages of conflict. After each unproductive conversation, James and Jen start to engage in *hostile mind reading*, where each attributes negative motivations to the other.[9]

If we let our daughter play on the team, James thinks, *she's afraid Kendra will become more attached to me than to her. Her insecurity is out of control.*

I've always had concerns about his spiritual maturity. He's using our daughter as an excuse to get out of going to church, Jen concludes.

While these concerns may have some legitimacy, Satan attempts to cast them in the most negative light possible by

adopting broad interpretations of each other. James is now seen
by Jen as being unspiritual, while Jen is viewed by James as insecure and financially tight-fisted.

Having adopted negative views of each other that obscure positive
qualities, they engage in *kitchen-sinking*, where in addition to the
original issue (daughter's participation on a travel team), a long list
of grievances that have accumulated over the course of the marriage
are also brought up. Subsequent conversations easily get sidetracked
by the insertion of past hurts and disappointments. One casualty
that occurs in this stage of the conversation is the absence of phatic
communication. *Emphatic* communication focuses on dramatic
events (discussing finances, kids' schedules, family commitments),
while *phatic* communication centers on daily, seemingly trivial interactions (playful banter, inside jokes, hugs) that foster connection.
What's often overlooked is that the small talk couples engage in sets
a positive tone for dramatic conversations. Since the disagreement
over the travel team started, playful moments between Jen and
James have gradually stopped. Now, all they do is go around and
around on issues that seemingly never get resolved.

SPIRITUAL IMPLICATIONS OF
MARITAL CONFLICT

The disagreement about the travel team has also created an opening
for spiritual forces to target James and Jen's view of God. Jen's disappointment with her husband putting sports above church commitment wears on her. Throughout the marriage, she has struggled
with his hot and cold interest toward spiritual topics. Slowly, that
disappointment has shifted toward God. *Why doesn't God do*

something? It's obvious that church should trump sports; why not make it obvious to James? Are you even paying attention, God? Conversely, James has always dreamed of his girls playing sports at a level he never achieved. He has always been drawn to stories of fathers making great sacrifices so their children can succeed. But finances and a resistant wife are threatening to close the door. *God knows exactly how much money we need to make this a reality. Why isn't he providing? Surely, he can't keep this opportunity from my daughter.* Slowly, God is seen as uncaring and inactive—a divine absent Father. This change of perspective plays into the devil's strategy of not only isolating them as a couple but moving them away from God. When each of them becomes aware of negative self-talk toward God, the evil one attempts to foster pangs of shame.

As the registration deadline arrives, James announces that his daughter *will* play, and he will work overtime to pay the registration. End of discussion. At night, they offer a perfunctory goodnight, but they are as distant as brothers on a hotel bed. A spiritual foothold has been established and systematically fortified by Satan.

READER   Wow, that's depressing!

AUTHOR   Sure. Spiritual battle should be sobering.

READER   No. It's not spiritual battle *per se* that is depressing, but how sneaky and successful Satan is. James and Jen never knew what hit 'em. That's not how I envisioned spiritual battle.

AUTHOR   How did you envision it?

READER   Well, something a lot more dramatic. After all, doesn't the Bible tell us that Satan is a roaring lion? The Satan you describe with both Adam and Eve and this couple is like a stealth ninja operating in the shadows. Who's right? You or the Bible?

AUTHOR   We both are.

READER   Elaborate, please.

AUTHOR   The Genesis narrative depicts the serpent as subtle (crafty), while Peter suggests Satan resembles a roaring lion (1 Pet 5:8). We have to be careful not to read too much into Peter's statement. His goal is to prompt us to be alert concerning the reality of spiritual battle. To do so, he evokes the most threatening image he can.

READER   A roaring lion.

AUTHOR   Correct. The reaction you would have learning that a lion is on the loose in your neighborhood is the same emotional response you should have to the devil stalking your marriage. Peter is not saying that Satan will necessarily attack like a ferocious lion but that he is a foe to be taken seriously. We can't expect a roar to precede every attack.

READER   You mean, he'll never attack frontally or make himself obvious?

AUTHOR   No. It is entirely possible he will do so. However, military strategists understand that a frontal attack has the potential to wake up your enemy and unintentionally fortify his or her defenses.

READER   Peter is trying to get our attention.

AUTHOR   Yes. But has he been successful? Are we alert?

READER   Well, how do we fight against a demonic ninja?

AUTHOR   That will be the subject of chapter five. If you let me
           continue.

READER   Proceed.

We are fascinated with ninjas. Over twenty-two thousand people
on Twitter label themselves *social media ninjas*. The term is co-opted
by everyone from marketers (sales ninjas) to mothers (mommy
ninjas).[10] The term *ninja* is the combination of complex Chinese
characters that can be translated "one trained in stealth" or "shadow
warrior." In feudal Japan, only the wealthy could afford expensive
samurai armor and weapons. These warriors took great comfort in
the fine craftsmanship of their armored protection. Not so with
ninjas, who were often recruited from small villages where the price
of armor was wildly out of reach. Ninjas eschewed armor in favor of
loose clothing that matched the time of day. Thus, black was only
worn at night, while dark blue or reddish colors were utilized at
dusk. The confidence of a ninja was not in his armor but in his
training. More important to these shadow warriors were their
knowledge, training, and character, rather than a helmet, breastplate,
or sword. In the end, samurai soldiers were no match for ninjas.

    When the apostle Paul commands us to "put on the full armor
of God" (Eph 6:11), is he urging us to be like a samurai arrayed in
armor or a ninja steeped in knowledge and training? The armor
Paul envisions mirrors a ninja in that protection comes from
knowledge and training rather than actual physical equipment to
be put on. While Satan may be ninja-like in his stealth tactics,
Christians adopt the attitude that our greatest strength comes from
clothing ourselves with spiritual truths that protect us from the
enemy. But how do we put on spiritual armor when we encounter

demonic forces? In chapter five, we discover spiritual truths that, if embraced, protect us from the stealth attacks of our adversary.

CONTINUING THE DISCUSSION

1. In an attempt to attack from the rear, D. G. Kehl asserts that Satan seeks to win a "minor" victory in preparation for the "big fall." What minor victories—harboring bad attitudes, out-of-control schedules, lack of couple's time, overspending, too much focus on kids—is Satan achieving in an attempt to secure a big fall in your marriage?

2. As you look at the history of your marriage, do you view God as being restrictive or generous? Are there things you feel God should have provided, but didn't? What criteria do you use to judge God's goodness? Are your criteria rooted in material goods (e.g., healthy bank account, ability to have kids, kids doing well, overall health) or spiritual blessings (e.g., forgiveness, certainty of heaven, Christ's ultimate sacrifice)?

3. If one of Satan's favorite tactics is to divide and conquer, what areas of your marriage are you divided on? What differences of opinion exist in your marriage that might lead to divisions if not attended to? What's the biggest difference of opinion that exists in your marriage currently?

4. If Jen and James came to you for advice about enrolling their daughter in a travel sports team, what advice would you give to them as a couple? What priorities or values would guide your counsel? If you spoke to each individually, how would you address James and Jen's individual fears?

5

FIGHTING BACK AS A COUPLE

UTILIZING OUR SPIRITUAL PROTECTION

You're ready!"

A pivotal time in martial arts training is when the instructor informs you that it's time to fight the black belts. Having watched these elite athletes train day after day, I was fully aware of what they are capable of—and the pain they can inflict.

"Today, you spar with the first-degree black belts," my instructor commanded.

Though I was trying to show my best poker face, he could tell I was nervous. After all, I was one of the oldest students. And let's face it, I drove to class in a minivan. If I survived this sparring, would I even make it to work the next day? A Bruce Lee protégée I was not.

"Don't worry, we provide protection," he said with a wry smile.

He helped me get dressed for this full-contact encounter by putting on shin guards, chest protector, cup, gloves, mouth guard, and helmet.

"See, got you covered head to toe. Go get 'em!"

Walking out to face my first black belt—a tall young man exhibiting a confident smirk—I felt a little better knowing that at least my vital organs were protected. I'll never forget the last words my instructor said as I bowed toward my opponent, "Remember, it's not the equipment that will protect you, it's your training. Begin!"

The apostle Paul takes the same attitude toward anxious Christians who are preparing to mix it up with demonic opponents. While he doesn't attempt to soft sell the seriousness of the encounter, he describes the protection—belt of truth, breastplate of righteousness, sandals of peace, shield of faith, helmet of salvation, sword of the Spirit—all believers should wear as we engage in spiritual warfare. The better we understand each level of protection the more we can confidently confront spiritual forces that threaten our marriages.

WELCOME TO THE WAR

Before Paul describes our spiritual protection, he reminds us of a pivotal truth—the greatest obstacle to cultivating a Christ-honoring marriage is not the differences between you and your spouse. Rather, the greatest "struggle" is against "spiritual forces of evil" (Eph 6:12) that seek to exploit those differences. It is a grave mistake, notes Paul, to *only* focus on the "flesh and blood" person before us when having marital difficulties. As discussed in chapter three, not all conflict is necessarily an indicator of spiritual oppression. However, Paul admonishes us that if we detect spiritual opposition then we must have a spiritual response. Ignoring demonic influence is "like treating the symptoms of a disease while ignoring its underlying causes," notes theologian Keith Ferdinando. "Worse than that, it encourages us to suppose that our spiritual combat is a humanly manageable enterprise."[1]

To convince us of the seriousness of the fight before us, Paul uses an athletic term, *struggle*. This term describes two people engaged in an intense wrestling match characterized by hand-to-hand combat where the goal is to forcefully pin a person down— often by wrapping arms around the opponent's neck—declaring victory. New Testament scholar Kenneth Wuest suggests that Paul's illustration takes on grave significance when we consider that in some extreme forms of Greek wrestling the loser "had his eyes gouged out with resulting blindness for the rest of his days."[2] If this form of wrestling is what Paul had in mind, it no doubt effectively garnered the attention of his readers. Wuest suggests it should also catch our attention: "The Christian's wrestling against the powers of darkness is no less desperate and fateful."[3]

Having been made aware of our desperate struggle against spiritual forces, Paul instructs us to get dressed for battle for when the "day of evil comes" (Eph 6:13). However, Christians should assume that the "day of evil" has already arrived and our struggle with spiritual forces is continuous. "It goes on throughout this age," notes Ferdinando, "every day and every minute of every day. There is no vacation, no weekend, no sabbatical, no home leave, no tea break."[4] Paul is clear, our preparation for battle is not some fad, and Christians cannot be content being weekend spiritual warriors. Resisting dark forces is not "a pastime, a game, or a hobby, but total warfare, and Satan does not respect our times of relaxation but exploits them."[5]

A MATTER OF THE HEART

Before we examine Paul's description of our spiritual armor, it is important to note two key differences between what I wore for sparring black belts and our spiritual protection. First, the shin guards, mouth piece, and chest protector I put on to fight a black belt were actual objects I could see and touch. I carry them with me in my sports bag and pull them out when needed. If I don't have the bag with me, I don't have my protection. Not so with our spiritual protection.

While Paul makes use of a Roman soldier dressed for battle as his model, the specific elements (belt of truth, breastplate of righteousness, helmet of salvation) are not actual objects, but rather a set of beliefs to adopt and, most importantly, live out. While it takes me minutes to put on my sparring gear, it may take years to fully adorn my spiritual armor. Our spiritual armor is not like water wings a mom puts on a child who can barely swim. Rather, our spiritual protection is proportional to how well we submerge ourselves in biblical truth.

Second, wearing a chest protector and head gear during sparring means I can be somewhat lax in blocking a kick; if I miss my block, protection saves me. The spiritual protection Paul offers does not provide partial protection. It will only work, as we will soon see, if we fully embrace becoming disciples of Christ.[6]

Before Paul addresses our spiritual armor, he prays for believers in Ephesus that the "the eyes of your heart may be enlightened" (Eph 1:18). The word *heart* in the New Testament does not merely mean emotions but also your intellect and will. Paul prays that your *entire* person will be radically transformed by God's truth.

God is not only concerned with how much you know, but how you are living out what you profess to believe. To be honest, many of us fail to live out what we already know. David Whitney, who writes about spiritual growth, observes that many Christians he meets are "a mile wide and an inch deep. There are no deep, time-worn channels of communing discipline between them and God. They have dabbled in everything but disciplined themselves in nothing."[7] We cannot dabble with the elements of our spiritual armor. Rather, they will take time, discipline, and deep introspection before full protection is given.

GETTING DRESSED

Be warned: utilizing God's armor requires asking ourselves probing questions. Clint Arnold summarizes the challenge of dressing in our spiritual armor by noting that "knowing the truth of how we are in union with Christ, cultivating the virtues of this new identity, and using the resources available through this new relationship are at the heart of what it means to put on the armor of God."[8] The first element of our protection challenges us to think about our relationship to truth. How truthful are you in dealing with yourself, others, and God?

Belt of truth. For a Roman soldier a belt was no mere accessory. It kept all parts of armor in place. Without it, his breastplate would slump and his sword would be inaccessible. Roman soldiers fully understood how essential the belt was for protection moving into battle. Paul agrees. His first instruction in dressing us for spiritual battle is to "stand firm then, with the belt of truth buckled around your waist" (Eph 6:14). Paul is not merely stating that our knowledge of God's truth (key doctrines or theological beliefs) should serve as our belt. As important as biblical truth is, he is equally interested in your personal relationship to truth. How often do you spin the truth to protect yourself? When needed, do you flat-out lie to get out of a bad situation?

In an age of rampant claims of fake news, how much have we bought into the habit of spinning the truth? According to researchers at the University of Massachusetts, many of us regularly lie when trying to appear competent. In their study, 60 percent of participants when fact-checked told at least one lie in a ten-minute conversation.[9] Many of us today feel so free to disregard or manipulate facts to make a point that the *Oxford English Dictionary* named *post-truth* the 2016 word of the year.[10] In other words, truth is subject to my feelings or personal beliefs. The ancient writers of the book of Proverbs would critique our embrace of the post-truth culture. In forceful language, they state that the "Lord detests lying lips" (Prov 12:22). While the righteous hate what is false, the liar becomes a stench to others (Prov 13:5). Once lying starts, lies pour out in increasing volume (Prov 14:5). Paul echoes these ancient writers and commands that we should "put off falsehood" and strive to "speak truthfully" to each other (Eph 4:25).

Why would Paul begin preparing us for spiritual battle by focusing on integrity and truth telling? J. Oswald Sanders speculates that truthfulness is "the unifying and strengthening factor in the life and experience of the Christian soldier. Was not Satan's first attack on the human race waged in the realm of truth? Did he not impugn the truthfulness of God?" Sanders encourages modern readers to be prepared for an attack from the father of lies. "He will tempt us to hypocrisy and insincerity, inciting us to untruth or half-truths."[11] In short, when we lie we speak the evil one's "native language" (Jn 8:44). Like trying to button a shirt after missing the first hole, failing to gird our waists with truth-telling will affect how subsequent pieces of armor fit.

What was Paul's inspiration for his description of spiritual armor? Was it exclusively a Roman soldier? If so, why did he leave out key pieces of equipment such as javelins or leg armor? Is it possible that Paul's primary source is not a Roman soldier but the Old Testament prophet Isaiah's depiction of God as a divine warrior? Isaiah states that "righteousness will be his belt and faithfulness the sash round his waist" (Is 11:5). He continues, "He put on righteousness as his breastplate, and the helmet of salvation on his head" (Is 59:17).* Most likely, Paul is utilizing both his observations of Roman soldiers—ever present in his day—with Isaiah's striking image of a divine warrior.

*For more of this perspective, see Clinton E. Arnold, *Ephesians*, Zondervan Exegetical Commentary on the New Testament (Grand Rapids: Zondervan, 2010), 420-23.

Breastplate of righteousness. After securing his belt, a Roman solider put on a brass breastplate, which would protect against fatal wounds. Soldiers were so fond of this piece of equipment they named it the "heart protector." Paul believes Christians need similar protection and commands us to put on a breastplate of righteousness. The type of righteousness Paul is concerned with has to do with our personal uprightness or moral character. Wuest notes the righteousness Paul describes is "sanctifying righteousness, the product of the Holy Spirit in the life of the yielded saint. It can be defined as moral rectitude."[12]

We all want others to see us as people of moral character. But are we? The Greek philosopher Plato had a unique test to measure a person's character. Plato would say to students, "Imagine I gave you a ring that when you put it on made you invisible to human sight. In what situations would you choose to wear it?" For Plato, the test would be to see if a person's words matched their actions. For example, you could tell your wife that you have strong convictions against watching movies that contain sexual content, yet when away from her simply slip on the ring and watch *any* movie undetected. You tell your spouse that you trust him, but slip on the ring to check text messages when he leaves his phone on the table. For Plato, virtue (integrity, character, trustworthiness, truthfulness) was not something you did only when people were watching; it was who you were when no one was watching. Like King David, we need to regularly ask of the Lord,

Search me, O God, and know my heart;
    try me and know my anxious thoughts.
See if there is any offensive way in me. (Ps 139:23-24)

Asking the Lord to search your heart is not for the faint of heart. How would you respond to the following?

- Do I really tell the truth to my spouse, or are they half-truths?
- Are there areas where I find it difficult to tell my spouse the truth?
- Am I trustworthy when it comes to issues of sexual temptation?
- Am I trustworthy when it comes to financial stewardship?

- Am I a person of my word? Do I usually follow through on what I say I'm going to do?

- Do I live out the values in private that I talk about in public?

- If I possessed Plato's ring, how would I use it?[13]

As various people have put it, our true character is revealed by how we behave when no one is watching. How much discrepancy is there between who I am in public and who I am in my private life?

Our introspection should also apply to our relationship with God. We can easily affirm to our spouse and children that God is a priority, but is he? To the church at Rome, Paul argues that all of us should make ourselves living sacrifices to God (Rom 12:1-2). "The problem with living sacrifices," humorously notes Christian educator Howard Hendricks, "is that they keep crawling off the altar."[14] How often do we boldly proclaim allegiance to Christ publically, while privately removing ourselves from the altar of sacrifice? At the heart of Plato's test is the idea that true character is manifested when no one is watching. When spiritual battle starts to heat up, our character will be revealed. While no one is perfect, the moral choices and habits we cultivate over time will serve as a vibrant defense against spiritual attack.

Feet fitted with gospel of peace. What most separated Roman soldiers from their adversaries were not superior tactics or weaponry. Surprisingly, it was their footwear. Their boots—called "caligal"—had spikes that allowed them to not only march at a fast pace but stand firm when defending against attacks. Once a Roman soldier got his feet planted, it was almost impossible to move him. Our spiritual armor also allows us to gain firm footing—with God.

Paul writes that our feet are not "fitted" with spikes, but with "the gospel of peace" (Eph 6:15).

As we have already observed, one of Satan's favorite tactics is not only turning spouses against each other but getting us to believe that God has turned against us. Is it possible, the evil one suggests, that God could get so fed up with our sin that he erupts in anger? Paul's answer is found in his concept of *lavished grace*. One of the key results of the gospel is that for those who embrace Christ, God extends never-ending grace. Paul informs us that in Christ we have both "redemption" and the "forgiveness of sins" (Eph 1:7). Redemption conveys the fact that we have been set free from the enslavement to sin by payment of a price. What was the cost of our freedom? In vivid language, Paul tells us it was through Christ's blood and sacrifice (v. 7). The result is that all of our sins—past, present, and future—have been forgiven. When Jesus died two thousand years ago, how many of our sins were in the future? Answer: all of them! As a result, all of our sins have been dealt with from God's perspective.

Is it possible—as Satan asserts—that God's patience or grace could run out as we fumble through life? No. Our peace with God is in "accordance with the riches of God's grace" which he "lavished on us" (Eph 1:7-8). The Greek word for "lavish" means "to exceed a number."[15] Imagine a numerical limit to God's grace. *If I look at pornography another twenty times, God will be done with me! If I lose my temper at the kids ten more times, God will lose his temper at me! If I neglect my wedding vows another year, God's patience will be exhausted.* The lavished grace Paul is describing exceeds *that* number. Two results follow. First, we are never to question the firm footing we have with God. Regardless of what Satan accuses, the possibility of God condemning his children has been removed (Rom 8:1).[16] Second, the lavished grace we have received is to be passed on to our spouses. "Be kind and compassionate to one another," asserts Paul, "forgiving each other, *just as* in Christ God forgave you" (Eph 4:32 emphasis added).

 The biblical concept of redemption comes from the Greek word *agorazo*, which means to *purchase in the marketplace*. During New Testament times, slaves were sold to the highest bidder in public auctions. That image is co-opted by New Testament writers to describe our salvation. As slaves to sin, we were bought by Christ—his bidding made public by the crucifixion—and set free from the bondage to a sinful life. Just as slaves were sold from one master to another, we too move from being oppressed by the evil one to becoming a willing slave of Christ. "Believers are not brought by Christ into a liberty of selfish ease. Rather, since they have been bought by God at terrible cost, they have become God's slaves, to do his will."*

*Leon Morris, *The Apostolic Preaching of the Cross*, 3rd ed. (Grand Rapids: Eerdmans, 1965), 54.

Shield of faith. While the confidence of Roman soldiers was well known, there was one weapon that struck fear even into these elite soldiers—fiery darts. The head of these darts were soaked in pitch and lit on fire. The psychological effect of being the bull's-eye for hundreds of flaming darts would have been unnerving. Even if a soldier's shield stopped the dart, the shield would catch fire. In one historical account, a Roman commander had over two hundred darts embedded in his

98   CHAPTER 5

shield and survived. Roman soldiers discovered that covering their
shields with a layer of animal hide would quench the dart if hit. Similarly, Paul warns his readers that they need to be on alert for flaming
arrows designed by the evil one to derail them. To counter this attack,
Paul charges us to take up the shield of faith (Eph 6:16).

The purpose of this spiritual shield is to "extinguish" the strategies of Satan before they spread. However, the strength of our
shield will be determined by the assuredness of our faith. Here,
unfortunately, many Christians are vulnerable. How stable is our
faith? How much security does our faith provide? Imagine you are
being chased by a mountain lion. To escape, you run into a wooden
shed and slam the door. As you retreat into a corner, you hear the
lion slamming against the door. Do you feel safe? It all depends on
the strength of the door. If it is termite infested and rotten, you
cower each time the door is attacked. However, if the door is steel
enforced, you can easily relax. Tragically, most Christians today
have no idea how strong the door of their faith is; thus, they cower
at *every* challenge. This uncertainty, over time, takes a toll.[17]

Today in terms of belief, more and more American adults place
themselves in the "none" category and no longer identify with a
religious group. Sadly, 78 percent of "nones" were raised in a religious family. According to Pew Research, those interviewed gave
the following reasons for leaving faith behind:

- Learning about evolution when I went to college.
- Rational thought makes religion go out the window.
- I just realized somewhere along the line that I didn't really believe it.
- Lack of evidence of a creator.[18]

Along with thousands of others, these nones concluded the door of faith was, in the end, flimsy. As a couple, what is your conclusion? While the need for faith will never be eliminated (Heb 11:6), Jesus called us to love him with all our heart, soul, and *mind* (Mt 22:37). What are the reasons you, as a couple, hold to faith? What questions make it difficult to believe? Over the past twenty-five years, I've trained Christians how to respond to doubts that challenge faith. Here are the most common challenges from audiences:

- Can God still be good in a world of pain and suffering?

- How can Christianity be the only way to God when Buddhists, Muslims, and Hindus are just as sincere in their faith as I am in mine?

- If Jesus is the only way to salvation, then what about the millions who have never heard of him?

- With so many different and often conflicting interpretations of the Bible, how can we really know what it says?

- Did God really command the armies of Israel to kill women and children? If so, why does he get a free pass?

Considering questions like these can be bewildering and, if we are honest, depressing. Understandably, many respond by setting their questions aside altogether. Yet, if we do not augment our commitment to Jesus with solid reasons for faith, are we only loving him with part of who we are? Over time, will it become more difficult to keep doubts or nagging questions at bay? Like those now identifying as nones, our faith starts to slowly die. While we do not need to quit our jobs and become professional apologists, our shield of faith grows in part by having solid reasons for our most cherished beliefs. To neglect tough questions as a couple is to give the evil one an opportunity to target our faith.[19]

Helmet of salvation. For a soldier, the need for a quality helmet is obvious. If a blow to the head occurred, the soldier would quickly become disorientated or worse. Through his use of fiery arrows, Satan seeks to equally disrupt and disorient us (Eph 6:16). Ancient church leaders such as Origen and Jerome interpreted these fiery arrows as the evil one's attempt to interject disrupting *thoughts* into the mind of believers.[20] To defend us, Paul commands us to put on the helmet of salvation to assure we keep the right perspective concerning our relationship to God. Time and again, Paul urges us to renew our minds with God's truth (Rom 12:2).

A central question for any Christian is, Who controls your thoughts? "The mind governed by the flesh is death," Paul asserts, while the "mind governed by the Spirit is life and peace" (Rom 8:6). Two questions follow from Paul's observation. First, are our lives marked by a deep-seated peace rooted in God's grace, love, and salvation? A love so firm, states Paul, that nothing can separate us from Christ's care (Rom 8:31-39). Second, how can our minds be controlled by the Spirit? Our last piece of protection addresses how the Spirit can assure right thinking.

Sword of the Spirit. While all weapons were important to a Roman infantryman, there was one that never left his side. While the long sword, called a *spatha*, was only carried into battle, the Roman short sword went everywhere with a solider, even when off duty. This short sword was sharp on both sides and could be used to attack and parry the thrusts of an enemy or local thief. For Christians, our spiritual short sword is the Word of God applied to our thinking by the Holy Spirit. When temptations or accusing thoughts are directed at us from the evil one, the Spirit counters by bringing to mind biblical truth. The writer of Hebrews tells us the Word of God is "alive and active." Sharper than a Roman short sword, it has the ability to judge "thoughts and attitudes of the heart" (Heb 4:12). The Spirit judges non-Christians guilty, but Christians are judged righteous and forgiven. But how much material do we give the Holy Spirit to work with in our personal lives or marriages? How much are spiritual practices like meditation and solitude, or even reading the Bible regularly, common in the flow of our marriage?

LifeWay Research surveyed over 2,900 Protestant churchgoers and discovered only 19 percent read the Bible daily. Those who read the Bible as part of a daily regime report frequent times of confession, deeper embracing of their forgiveness, making obedience to God a priority, praying for others, and a heightened focus on spiritual growth.[21] Can we realistically expect the Spirit to bring to mind Scripture if we have not saturated ourselves in biblical truth?

ASSESSING OUR SPIRITUAL PROTECTION

Based on Paul's description of spiritual armor, how protected are you? To help gauge your individual protection, consider the following questions.

Belt of truth. How often do I spin the truth with others? If people would fact-check what I say, what would they discover? Are there areas of my personal life where I never fully disclose what's going on? Do I subscribe to my own version of post-truth?

Breastplate of righteousness. Am I a trustworthy person? Are the values I espouse in public the ones I live out at home? Am I a person of my word? How am I most tempted to use Plato's ring of invisibility? How often do I ask God to search my heart?

Gospel of peace. Do I believe that God lavishes me with grace? Could I ever exhaust God's grace? What sin do I struggle with that tempts me to think God could turn his back on me if I don't stop?

Shield of faith. Do I have good reasons for what I believe? Is the door of my faith firm enough to sustain a challenge? What doubts do I have? Am I embarrassed by my doubts? Has my pride kept me from sharing doubts with others? Is my faith in God growing or becoming stagnant?

Helmet of salvation. Do I have deep-seated peace that God loves me? Could anything separate me from God's love? How much does the Spirit influence my thinking? How often do I slip back into old thought patterns?

Sword of the Spirit. How often do I read the Bible? Do I regularly take time to meditate on biblical truth, allowing the Spirit to enlighten it in a personal way? Have I ever read the Bible cover to cover?

GETTING DRESSED AS A COUPLE

Assessing your own personal spiritual protection is only half the equation. In using a Roman soldier as his model, Paul would have been acutely aware of what Roman armies were known for—fighting as a unit. Before recruits were handed a weapon, they were taught to march and think as a unit. Each step they took was in unison, or punishment from trainers came swiftly. Commanders understood that stragglers who broke formation in the heat of battle put everyone at risk. It was drilled into a soldier that his chances of survival depended on acting in concert with the men on his left and right. To be out of sync was a matter of life and death.

The same principle applies to the spiritual protection of your marriage. It is not enough to merely focus on your own spiritual protection. Like a Roman soldier, the level of protection of your spouse directly affects you, and vice versa. Your lack of telling the truth not only affects personal intimacy with God but disrupts the level of trust in the marriage. Your lack of confidence in God bleeds into your decision making as a couple. You cannot hide behind your spouse's shield of faith. When one person is weak, it makes both of you vulnerable. How would you evaluate your marriage as a fighting unit in relation to God's protection? As a couple consider the following.

Belt of truth. Are there areas of our marriage where we don't feel the freedom to be truthful? Do we punish each other when truth is spoken? When we speak truth to each other, is it all truth and no love? Or are we so insecure about our marriage that we only extend love and never speak truth?

Breastplate of righteousness. What level of trustworthiness exists in our marriage? As a couple, do we regularly place ourselves on the altar of self-sacrifice, or are we continually crawling off to do our own thing?

Gospel of peace. Do we regularly extend grace to each other? Are we compassionate to others? Do we extend the same grace to ourselves? Has God's lavished grace made us more forgiving of the faults of each other?

Shield of faith. As a couple, is our faith becoming more mature in all aspects (heart, soul, mind)? Have we become stagnant in our faith? What steps of faith have we taken lately? What doubts about

God's goodness or provision have we experienced as a couple? Do we have faith that God is still at work in our marriage? What examples could we list of God's provisions?

Helmet of salvation. How much as a couple does the Spirit influence our decisions? What makes it easy to believe the best about my spouse? What makes believing the best about my spouse difficult?

Sword of the Spirit. As a couple, how do we spend our evenings? Do we binge-watch Netflix or spend time reading the Bible together? How much do we encourage each other to not only read the Scriptures but meditate on them? What changes do we need to make in our daily schedule to free up time to read and reflect on God's Word?

The last part of our spiritual protection is not modeled after a Roman solider. It is unique to spiritual warfare and holds the key to our success. We are told to do it *in* the spirit and on *all* occasions. Paul even asks that we do it for him as he fights on. The last element of our protection—prayer—is the subject of chapter six.

INTERVIEW: SPIRITUAL PROTECTION

Clint Arnold is a world-class New Testament scholar who specializes in the topic of spiritual warfare. Not only did he write the foreword to this book but his own writings and input—over many cups of coffee—have been invaluable. He specializes in how the apostle Paul approaches the topic of spiritual opposition and the advice he gives believers on how to protect ourselves.

TIM   After all your study of Paul and the New Testament, what do you think is Satan's favorite go-to tactic?

CLINT   The first thing he does is to cause us to question our standing with God. This is not a surprise because *diabolos* (the devil) means "accuser." Central to the apostle Paul's teaching is that we have received righteousness as a free gift from God. Not all is lost if we have messed up, even badly. Because this righteousness is a gift, we are always in good standing with God. He will never reject us.

TIM   How does Satan try to undermine that truth?

CLINT   All of us—on occasion—fall back into sin. Satan seeks to exploit that struggle. "Who are you trying to kid? You call yourself a Christian? You don't deserve God's love and grace!" And you know what, we don't! But, we have it regardless of how much we struggle.

TIM   When in the midst of struggling with stubborn sins, it's easy to forget how much Jesus loves us.

CLINT   Absolutely. We are prime targets for Satan's lies. I was recently talking to a man who fell back into a porn habit. You could see the shame etched all over his face. I decided to ask an odd question. "If Jesus walked into this office right now, what reaction would he have toward you? He knows all about your struggles with porn. How do you think he should treat you?"

TIM   Wow! How did he respond?

CLINT   He told me he thought Jesus would turn away. Jesus wouldn't want *anything* to do with him. When he said this, I almost jumped out of my chair. Jesus would give you the biggest bear hug you could imagine, I said! This poor man was susceptible to the evil one because he was not clothing himself with what Paul calls the belt of truth. We have to see ourselves as God sees us! Listen to God's truth over Satan's lies.

TIM   I'm glad you mentioned a part of our spiritual armor.

CLINT   Sounds like you could have used some actual armor when you fought the black belts (laughing).

TIM   Ouch. Don't remind me. What should we keep in mind as we utilize the spiritual armor described by Paul?

CLINT   Don't overdramatize spiritual warfare. Satan is not like a bogeyman who only shows up when people play with Ouija boards. He is much subtler than that! He looks for small openings and seeks to exploit them.

TIM   Like anger.

CLINT   Exactly. We all get angry. Satan is looking for a type of anger that can be cultivated into a grudge or bitterness. Before we know it, he's got a foothold. Next, putting on our spiritual armor necessarily entails practicing spiritual disciplines like prayer, fasting, Bible reading, meditating on God's truth.

TIM   Kind of like eating your spiritual fruits and veggies.

CLINT   That's right. The simple rule of spiritual battle is that the closer we are to Jesus, the more protected we'll be.

TIM   I was hoping it would be more like the Power Rangers who say, "It's morphin' time! Unleash the power!" when they head into a fight.

CLINT   Nope. The armor of God is a lifestyle of pursuing God, not a superhero trick.

TIM   Any part of the armor of God you think believers most neglect?

CLINT   It is extremely important to, as Paul says, "pray in the Spirit." In part, that means asking the Spirit to alert us to spiritual attack and impress on us how Satan may be tempting us individually or as a couple.

TIM   What would that sound like?

CLINT   If you and your spouse are having an unusually intense disagreement, it may be wise to call a time out and ask the Spirit to reveal if spiritual forces are at play seeking to drive a wedge between you. Ask for specific insight into how the evil one might be seeking to exploit emotions, fears, or anger. If the answer is *no*, then you get about doing the hard work of resolving the differences. If yes, then develop a plan.

TIM   Like buying this book!

CLINT   I was thinking a plan that includes humbly praying together for the Spirit's help.

TIM   Oh, that too! (smiling)

CONTINUING THE DISCUSSION

1. As a spouse, how would you assess your own spiritual protection? What areas is your spiritual armor most vulnerable to attack? What concrete steps might you take individually to shore up your armor?

2. As a couple, how would you assess your spiritual protection? What areas are most vulnerable to attack? How well do you work as a team to equip yourselves in each aspect of your spiritual armor?

3. Being fitted with the gospel of peace means we experience
   God's lavished grace, which can never be exhausted. As a
   couple, do you believe this biblical truth (Eph 1:7-8)?
   What specific sin committed by your spouse tempts you
   to withhold grace?

4. According to Arnold, praying in the Spirit means asking the
   Spirit to alert us to spiritual attack and impress on us how
   Satan may be tempting us individually or as a couple. How
   often as a couple do you ask the Spirit to alert you to possible spiritual attack? If seldom, what hinders you from
   seeking the Spirit's perspective?

6

OUR GREATEST DEFENSE: PRAYER

ENERGIZING OUR SPIRITUAL PROTECTION

I hear the intruders coming up the stairs.

With each heavy thud, they get closer to our bedroom. I get out of bed and stand by the door; fists raised and heart pounding. I have the strongest feeling that they aren't here to steal anything but rather to hurt my wife and me. *If they come through the door, I need to attack first. Take them out one by one and hope they don't have weapons.* I brace for the door to open. It never does. Slowly, reason overtakes fear. Why didn't our dog bark? How did they bypass the alarm system? Why is my wife still sleeping? I slowly open the door and look out into a dark and empty hallway. Was I dreaming? It felt so real. With heart still racing and drops of sweat coming down my forehead, I slip back under the covers.

The next night, it happened again.

Three days before the dreams started I had agreed to serve as the interim teaching pastor at a church in Orange County, California, as they searched for a senior pastor. My wife and I equally felt that we should serve in this capacity *and* that this was going to make us a target for spiritual attack. The violent dreams were an unnerving confirmation that we were right on both counts.

When the dreams started, we felt a sense of urgency to utilize the spiritual protection described in chapter five. But how? The problem with spiritual armor is it is not like an actual chest protector or helmet we put on and forget about. Rather, our spiritual protection is the daily practice of drawing near to God and embracing biblical truth. How do we draw near to God in times of spiritual battle? "Submit yourselves, then, to God," advises James. "Resist the devil, and he will flee from you" (Jas 4:7). He continues, "Come near to God and he will come near to you" (v. 8). The main way we move toward God is through prayer. "Nothing accomplishes as much as prayer," notes author Kenneth Boa, "it is the means by which we lay hold of our strength in the Lord."[1]

As the violent dreams continued, what help could Jesus' tutorial on prayer give to counter this frightening form of spiritual attack?

JESUS' PRAYER AND SPIRITUAL BATTLE

If prayer is, as Kenneth Boa suggests, the means by which we lay hold of God's strength, then are we praying as Jesus did? As we consider Jesus' tutorial on prayer, we will specifically consider it through the lens of spiritual battle and the armor of God described in chapter five. Such a focus is warranted since his model prayer culminates with the sobering request, "deliver us from the evil one" (Mt 6:13).[2]

"This then, is how you should pray," Jesus begins. The purpose of the prayer, in part, is to challenge how we think about our priorities. Church statesmen and author John Stott notes that we can easily repeat Jesus' words like a parrot, with little introspection. Yet Jesus' prayer is designed to pull us away from our own self-interests. "We are constantly under pressure," notes Stott, "to conform to the self-centeredness of secular culture." The prayer we are about to consider is a revolution against the devil's attempts to influence our priorities. "In the Christian counter-culture our top priority concern is not our name, kingdom, and will, but God's priorities."[3] The opening of this prayer directly counteracts one of Satan's favorite strategies.

Our Father in heaven. "Perhaps the most frequent and insistent attack from Satan to which we are vulnerable is accusation," notes Neil T. Anderson in his book *The Bondage Breaker*.[4] As evidenced in the Garden, the evil one consistently insinuates that God does not have our best interests in mind. The reason this accusation gets traction is that we often compare God to imperfect human fathers. Or perhaps a father who loved us but lacked resources to adequately care for us. Jesus starts his prayer as a preemptive strike against any attempt to undermine our confidence in God's love or provision. Jesus is careful to communicate that God is not "the kind of father we sometimes read about or hear about—autocrat, playboy, drunkard—but he himself fulfills the ideal of fatherhood in his loving care for his children."[5]

When I address students who come from difficult families, I ask them to describe the characteristics of an *ideal* father. *Kind, loving, present, generous, compassionate, mature, responsible*, and *provider* are some of the most common descriptors. When my students respond with those words, they mirror Jesus' opening line: "Our Father [kind, loving, compassionate, mature, responsible] in heaven [generous, provider]." Thus Jesus "combines fatherly love with heavenly power, and what his love directs his power is able to perform."[6]

When we begin our prayers by affirming "Our Father in heaven," we are putting on what Paul describes as the "helmet of salvation" and the boots of "peace." By addressing God as Father, we affirm the right relationship afforded to us by the gospel. With God there is no longer any condemnation (Rom 8:1) but rather compassion, forgiveness, and lavished grace. King David boldly states in Psalm 103 that for those under God's mercy there is not only forgiveness of all sins (v. 3), but God himself crowns us with love and compassion (v. 4). David tenderly suggests that "as a father has compassion on his children" so does the Lord have compassion on us (v. 13). To think that God compassionately feels toward me the way I feel about my three sons is overwhelming. No matter what they do, I will always love them. The start of Jesus' prayer is not meant to be a type of etiquette in addressing the divine but rather a powerful means of rebutting the devil's flaming arrows of accusation. With our helmet of salvation firmly in place and our footing with God secured by sandals fitted with the peace of the gospel, we are properly suited to continue.

Hallowed be your name. To hallow something means to treat it as sacred and to honor it. Theologian R. T. Kendall suggests it is, in essence, to make a pledge that subsequently makes us accountable. "If I pray for God's name to be treated as holy, yet have no regard for manifesting holiness in my own life, I am a hypocrite."[7] One of my sons was a gifted high school basketball player who got into the habit of regularly assessing technical fouls during games. After yet one more technical foul, we had to have a talk. "What's on the back of your jersey?" I asked. "My last name," he replied. "No," I countered, "*our* last name." I explained that when he played he did not just represent himself or the high school, but the Muehlhoff family name. I then asked him to honor (hallow) our name by conducting himself in a way that reflected our family values.

The same is true when we seek to bring honor to God's name. Hallowing God's name in this way mirrors the *belt of truth* (truth telling) and the *breastplate of righteousness* (right living) central to the armor of God. Regularly praying that God's name will be hallowed *and* taking steps to make him sacred in our daily lives severely limits Satan's ability to tempt us.

Your kingdom come, your will be done, on earth as it is in heaven. During this part of the prayer we learn an interesting fact about God. Through his own choice, he does not force his will or kingdom on others. The Greek term for "will" is *thelēma*, which, in part, focuses on God's desire.[8] While God may desire that our planet is a place that mirrors the qualities of heaven—love, shalom, harmony—we know that signs of rebellion exist everywhere. "The planet Earth and its immediate surroundings," observes Dallas Willard, "seem to be the only place in creation where God permits his will to be *not* done."[9] A key part of Jesus' prayer is that God's kingdom will first invade our lives and then drench our surroundings. Specifically, our marriages should be pockets of God's kingdom in our neighborhoods and cities. Knowing that a key purpose of your marriage is to advance his kingdom rather than accomplish some version of the American Dream—constant upward mobility, secure bank account, happiness—helps keep our relational house in order.

For over twenty-seven years my wife, Noreen, and I have spoken at marriage conferences. Often this includes speaking in our own hometown. Soon, word gets out that we are marriage experts. While we laugh at that label and do not take it seriously, those around us do. I will never forget sitting at one of my boy's baseball games and a stranger sat down next to us. "My wife and I just separated," he said in a loud tone. "I know you speak about marriage. Will you pray for us?" Though I had never met him before, he knew us. No doubt, everyone in the small stands heard his plea.

We shirk the idea that we are marriage experts because Noreen and I struggle as much as anyone. Having a PhD in relational communication does not help a lick, unless I am willing to apply it. On many occasions I don't. But knowing that others are watching us helps us understand our marriage is about something bigger. It is about displaying God's kingdom and being a ray of hope for others. The same is true of your marriage. In today's divorce culture, every year you stay together your credibility grows and your marriage— though not perfect—communicates volumes to those around you. Regularly praying "your kingdom come" not only helps keep our priorities straight but shields us from buying into culture's distorted value system.

Praying that "your kingdom come" also requires that we utilize our shield of faith. As scenes of suffering and evil dominate our news, can we still believe that God is good? Is he really at work in a world seemingly spiraling out of control? "The only thing you can say about God," quips Woody Allen, "is that he's an underachiever." While answers are hard to come by, one thing is clear— we live in a world filled with pain. Yet as Christians we believe God is good, enters our pain, and is deeply committed to us. Our faith in God's goodness must be rooted in something. As a couple, what grounds your faith that God's kingdom is in fact advancing? Every time a non-Christian friend comes to faith in Jesus, a struggling couple makes the courageous choice not to call it quits, or your own marriage sees signs of spiritual growth, we see evidence of God's kingdom advancing. In a world filled with so much darkness, we need to be constantly on the lookout for examples of God's invading kingdom.

In the next section of Jesus' prayer there is a shift from *your* to *us* and *our*. Once our focus toward God has been reestablished, we now have the freedom to focus on our needs and the needs of those around us. "God not only wants what is best for us by asking us to focus first on Him; He shows He cares about our daily struggles by focusing on our daily needs."[10] However, we will soon see that how we define "daily bread" opens us to spiritual attack.

Give us today our daily bread. In considering this request, some theologians have spiritualized it to define *bread* as spiritual nourishment. However, there is no reason to think God does not recognize that as physical and emotional beings, we need nourishment of all kinds. God understands that seeking to hallow his name and advance his kingdom requires sustenance. Daily bread, then, most certainly refers to "physical needs, emotional needs, material needs—every need not specifically mentioned in the petitions of the Lord's Prayer."[11] Should we bother God with trivial matters such as paying our rent, maintaining a car, finding like-minded friends, having adequate clothing, keeping a budget, maintaining patience with teenagers, and so forth? Choosing to "not bother God with such trivialities is as great an error as to allow trivialities to dominate our prayers."[12]

When Jesus suggests we pray for daily bread, many think he is referencing the children of Israel who relied on daily portions of manna given during their wilderness wanderings. The manna would rot at the day's end, making it impossible to hoard God's provision. For Americans, the temptation to hoard is great. In the 2017 movie *All the Money in the World*, billionaire J. Paul Getty (played by Christopher Plummer) refuses to pay a seventeen-million-dollar ransom demand for his kidnapped grandson. When it comes to light that he earns the sum of the ransom demand in one afternoon's earnings, he responds that currently he can't spare that kind of money. "How much money do you need?" inquires an employee. "One more dollar than I have now," Getty infamously responds.[13] While few of us can relate to having such wealth at our disposal, we all can feel the desire to protect what we have! Praying for daily needs is resistance to a culture that not only hoards but continually feeds a desire for just a little more—*more* money, *more* space, and *more* status.

Forgive us our debts. The phrase "forgive us our debts, as we also have forgiven our debtors" seems to imply a tit-for-tat relationship where my sins are forgiven in proportion to forgiving others. Is that the type of reciprocal relationship Jesus wishes to affirm? No. Jesus is informing us that the greatest indicator of truly embracing God's total forgiveness is our desire and capacity to forgive others! Theologian Mike Wilkins nicely summarizes Jesus' intention: "This does not teach that humans must forgive others before they can receive forgiveness themselves; rather, forgiveness of others is proof that that disciple's sins are forgiven and he or she possesses salvation."[14] Our ability to forgive others is perhaps our greatest defense against Satan's attempt to create footholds in our lives. Many theologians believe that harboring bitterness or refusing to forgive is what *most* opens us to demonic influence and footholds.[15] In light of this, Jesus immediately transitions from forgiveness to temptation.

 What footholds are created by refusing to forgive? Researchers note that choosing not to forgive others has dire physical, emotional, mental, and spiritual consequences. *Physical*: resentment creates a chemical imbalance in the hormones that makes us susceptible to disease while weakening the entire immune system. *Mental*: mental consequences include depression and an increase of stress hormones in the body. *Emotional*: hating someone causes us to become fixated on the individual in question, depleting the ability to focus on the emotional needs of others. *Spiritual*: Scripture flatly states that we cannot fully love God while hating another person (1 Jn 4:20).

Lead us not into temptation, but deliver us from the evil one. This last request takes on an ominous tone when we consider that the verb *deliver* carries with it the idea of snatching something in immediate danger. "The idea here is that the devil is constantly luring us into pits, snares of moral destruction, and being saved from them is beyond mere human willpower. Only God's watching and snatching and saving can save us."[16] For this reason, Jewish rabbis advocated starting each morning and evening with a prayer aimed at unveiling the devil's temptations.

Bring me not into the power of sin,
And not into the power of guilt,
And not into the power of temptation,
And not into the power of anything shameful.[17]

Jesus' prayer is a stark reminder of the self-centered, feeble prayers I offer. Rather than centering on my relationship with God, hallowing his name, asking his kingdom to advance, examining my willingness to forgive, and seeking protection from demonic tempting, I start every prayer with my career, health concerns, current book project, and needs of my wife and children. In other words, I begin with "daily needs" while skipping a kingdom perspective designed to protect. Sadly, such prayers ultimately fail to energize my spiritual armor, leaving my marriage and me open to attack.

PRAYING WITH AUTHORITY

Trained as an anthropologist, Charles Kraft spent a lifetime observing diverse people groups. Over time he became convinced of two realities. First, the struggle against dark powers transcends borders and ethnicity. Second, followers of Christ have the power to ward off these powers, but they seldom utilize their God-given authority to do so. After publishing more than twenty books on the subject and teaching at leading seminaries, Kraft is seen as an expert in the area of spiritual battle. His years of experience have led him to develop a view of spiritual authority that is essential to counteracting spiritual opposition through prayer.

To explain his view, Kraft appeals to something most of us use on a daily basis—a credit card. As he was preparing to go to college, his son came to him with a request. Could his name be added to his father's credit card? Kraft agreed and his son's name was added, giving him full financial authority. The same is true with Jesus. "When Jesus came to earth, it was as if He carried a credit card from His Father with the Father's name at the top and His own name under it."[18] During his ministry, Jesus never lost sight of where his authority resided. "By myself I can do nothing," Jesus declared (Jn 5:30). Kraft points out that two qualifications followed. Jesus had full authority to spend "whatever was in the Father's account so long as He kept on good terms with the Father and spent it for purposes of which the Father approved."[19] After his resurrection, Jesus shocks his disciples by passing on his authority to them. Jesus promises his disciples that they will receive power via the Holy Spirit (Acts 1:8). Today, Jesus transfers the same power and authority to us. "As Christians we have no choice as to whether or not we possess this authority. It comes in the package when the Holy Spirit is given to us."[20] Upon our conversion, our names were automatically added to Christ's credit card. But how do we access this spiritual line of credit?

Kraft notes there are two types of authority. *Status authority* is attached to us in our roles as marriage partners, parents, aunts and uncles, bosses, teachers, pastors, church leaders, Sunday school teachers, student resident advisers on a dormitory floor, and so forth. "We grant such people, for better or worse, the authority to set standards and influence us in a multitude of ways."[21] For married couples, status authority is crucial in the fight against demonic influence. Spouses have unique status to fully utilize Jesus' authority and power as we intercede for each other through prayer. If you determine—using the criteria established in previous chapters—that demonic influence is targeting your spouse, you can have full confidence that opposition *must* recognize and respond to your prayers. For example, when my wife started speaking publically at marriage conferences, she experienced a serious case of nervousness. Not having a background in public speaking, it was expected that she would have waves of anxiety. However, as her first conference approached, she started to question her worth. "What do I have to offer a ballroom of people? Who would want to listen to me?" As her husband, I used Jesus' authority and prayed, "In the power invested to me as Noreen's husband, I rebuke any dark powers. As her husband, I reject any attempt to undermine her as a child of God and attack her confidence. I command you to be silent." That's it.

If Jesus has truly delegated his power to me, I do not need to give a half-hour speech to demonic influences. My dad raised three rambunctious boys. While he was mostly fine with our rough-housing, there were times when it crossed a line. "Enough" was all he needed to say. He did not need to sit us down and make a case for his parental authority. He was the dad, we weren't. One word sufficed. Case closed. In certain situations, we have the same power. Kraft concludes, "I believe that the head of a home and the head of a church are automatically given a kind of spiritual authority by God as an inherent part of their status."[22] Does that mean I can only intercede for those over whom I have some type of status? Am I powerless to intervene for friends, neighbors, or coworkers? No.

The second type of authority is what Kraft labels *personal intimacy authority*. This type of authority comes not from position but an intimate relationship with Jesus. "As we stay connected to the Lord, we gain the authority that personal intimacy brings, and we learn to use that authority in the right manner."[23] The only condition for this type of authority is to be in proper relationship to the source of authority—Jesus. "I am the vine," Jesus tells his disciples, "you are the branches. If you remain in me and I in you, you will bear much fruit" (Jn 15:5). While Christ's love for us will never waver, our ability to exercise authority in praying for friends, coworkers, and neighbors can be compromised by sin. Just as my father's authority could be compromised by abusively forcing me and my brothers to stop messing around, our authority in Christ can be equally compromised by yielding to the deeds of the flesh. From the teachings of Kraft one thing is clear, followers of Christ have—either by position or association with Christ—authority to push back dark influences by utilizing prayer.

In his bestselling book *The Adversary*, Mark Bubeck argues that the forces of darkness respond to a believer's authority because they themselves are subject to authority.* Appealing to Ephesians 6, Bubeck asserts that Satan is the commander-in-chief and supreme strategist. Immediately under him are "principalities" and princes, such as the prince of Persia mentioned in Daniel 10. The next level is composed of "powers," which are less powerful than princes but can still pose great harm to believers. The organizational chart continues with "rulers of darkness," who could be compared to sergeants in an army. Under their command are beings described as "spiritual wickedness." These spiritual beings are foot soldiers who are most likely to be in direct contact with believers. These beings are numerous, as evidenced by a whole legion dwelling in one lone man (Mk 5:9).

*Mark I. Bubeck, *The Adversary: The Christian Versus Demon Activity* (Chicago: Moody Publishers, 2013).

WARFARE PRAYERS

Many find the idea of warfare prayers to be intimidating. "I have no idea what one sounds like" is a common response. A couple of points may be helpful. First, the model prayer offered by Jesus could be considered a type of warfare prayer. In order to be delivered from the "evil one" we need to embrace our proper relation to God (*our Father*) who has all authority (*in heaven*), deserves to be honored (*hallowed be your name*) and his agenda advanced (*your kingdom come*). We can be confident God will provide daily physical, relational, and spiritual needs (*give us our daily bread*). Our ability to forgive is evidence that we have embraced God's forgiveness (*as we also have forgiven our debtors*). Together, these spiritual truths protect us from temptation and the traps of the evil one (*but deliver us*). Once we place ourselves in the center of these biblical truths, we can offer prayers to counter specific challenges.

Second, when it comes to prayer many of us are self-taught. Rather than learning from others, we offer impromptu prayers on the go. The first step to crafting warfare prayers is to learn from others. Known as the apostle to Ireland, St. Patrick was a fifth-century British missionary credited with bringing Christianity to Ireland. His evangelistic zeal engendered extreme spiritual opposition. Tradition tells us that to offer himself and others protection, he wrote a prayer that has come to be known as St. Patrick's Breastplate. This prayer has not only encouraged believers throughout the centuries but is a model to us as we consider crafting our own warfare prayers. It reads in part:

> I bind unto myself today the power of God to hold and lead,
> His eye to watch, His might to stay, His ear harken to my need;

The wisdom of my God to teach, His hand to guide, His
shield to ward,
The Word of God to give me speech, His heav'nly host to be
my guard.
Against all Satan's spells and wiles, against false words of
heresy,
Against the knowledge that defiles, against the heart's
idolatry,
Against the wizard's evil craft, against the death-wound and
the burning,
The choking wave, the poison'd shaft, protect me Christ, till
Thy returning.[24]

Notice that St. Patrick's prayer pays keen attention to the three great enemies of every believer (world, flesh, and devil). The "knowledge that defiles" and the "poison'd shaft" represent an Irish culture that at the time was built on pagan beliefs, warfare, and slavery (world). The "heart's idolatry" centered on improper desires (flesh). Finally, "Satan's spells and wiles" are addressed (devil).

Our prayers should equally focus on the same concerns. After being tutored by the prayers of Jesus and St. Patrick, try creating your own. Here are some I have created over the years, which can easily be adapted.

Countering the world. "Our Father in heaven, thank you that as a couple our worth is in you. We reject our culture's narrative that self-worth is tied to status, power, and the constant desire for more. Help us to set our minds on things of the Spirit (Rom 8:5). We reject the devil's temptation to place our agenda above your kingdom's agenda. We reject the devil's attempt to make us see our marriage as a contract rather than a selfless covenant. In full authority, I intercede for my spouse and family, rejecting any false cultural narrative."

Concerning the flesh. "Our Father in heaven, we thank you for your unconditional love and forgiveness (Rom 5:1). We are dearly loved children despite our shortcomings. We welcome the conviction of the Spirit, while rejecting any feelings of shame. Help us to forgive ourselves and others as you have forgiven us. Let us present our lives as instruments of righteousness (Rom 6:13). In full authority, I intercede for my spouse and family, rejecting any feelings of shame for shortcomings."

Concerning the devil. "Our Father in heaven, help us as a couple to fully utilize our spiritual armor (Eph 6:13-18). Give us discernment to distinguish between normal marital disagreements and spiritual opposition. Today, let us draw near to you through prayer. As we seek to live out kingdom principles, keep us alert to our adversary. In full authority, I pray for my spouse and me to be adorned with spiritual armor and that the devil abandon current attacks."

If God has provided us protection via spiritual armor and prayer, why are Christians often so susceptible to attacks by forces of evil? We are most vulnerable when we forget that Jesus' model prayer and Paul's description of spiritual armor are never meant to be used in isolation from other believers. "Our Father in heaven" begins Jesus' model prayer. Asking for daily needs, forgiveness, and deliverance from evil are all present in the plural form. Prayer is most effectively done in community. Similarly, Paul's description of spiritual protection is contained in a letter presented not to an individual but to a community of believers in Ephesus. Paul ends his letter by exhorting readers to "be alert" as they intercede for each other (Eph 6:18). Our alertness will be greatly enhanced by standing shoulder to shoulder to face our adversary.

INTERVIEW: PRIMACY OF PRAYER

Marla Campbell is in her sixties and has spent a lifetime doing two things: teaching students and traveling the world telling others about Jesus. As a professor she has financial security and the admiration of her students. However, God apparently has other plans. He's made it clear to Marla that her second chapter involves leaving the security of the university to become a full-time missionary to Europe!

MARLA   I went from financial security to having to raise money for all my expenses. I felt God was asking me to take a giant faith leap off a cliff!

TIM   Stating the obvious, I imagine this decision has produced anxiety.

MARLA   You are good! (laughing). Yes! But God's message was clear: "If I took care of you in your thirties, I can take care of you now. Time to jump!"

TIM   Referring to Jesus' prayer, if he provided "daily bread" in the past, he'll do it today.

MARLA   Yes!

TIM   In addition to normal fears of a career change, any signs of spiritual battle?

MARLA   When I first felt God's leading, I also immediately felt the enemy come at me like a flood. "You are crazy to leave such a secure job! At your age, how are you going to raise money to cover salary and health insurance? Your students are going to forget you as soon as you leave!" One thing I've learned about the evil one is that he picks the aspects of God's calling that require most faith—raising support, leaving students I adore—and uses those very things to attack you!

TIM   In a sense, he finds your Achilles' heel and targets it.

MARLA   Without a doubt! Even though I'm single, my weak spot is the same as the couples reading this book—finances. At my age am I really going to raise enough money to live on? It's scary and the evil one can smell fear a mile away. Again, referring to Jesus' prayer, this is how the evil one is trying to "lead me into temptation."

TIM   How did you combat these spiritual attacks?

MARLA   Prayer and a good prayer partner. Praying, "Do not lead me into temptation" is so much easier with a prayer partner. My friend Sandy reminds me, "You can't keep birds from flying over your head, but you can keep them from making a nest in your hair!" In other words, it's my decision if I allow the evil one to get a foothold!"

TIM   Being bald, it's hard to relate.

MARLA   (smiling) Sorry. Didn't mean to be insensitive.

TIM   (laughing) How does prayer help keep the birds from nesting?

MARLA   I pray through Scripture as soon as these fears come. My favorite is Paul's admonition "Be anxious for nothing, but in everything by prayer" (Phil 4:6). I pray that throughout the day in order to take my thoughts captive. As soon as fear starts to surface, I combat them with a simple prayer—"Be anxious for nothing, be anxious for nothing, be anxious for nothing!"

TIM   Back to the importance of someone praying with you. Right?

MARLA   I regularly check in with my prayer partner to give her updates on fundraising as well as the intensity of spiritual pushback. Her response often is, "Just remember that Jesus is telling you not to look to your right or left. Rather, keep looking right into my face! I got you!"

TIM   Any last thought you'd share with couples reading this book?

MARLA   Are we letting Satan build a nest in our hair through harboring doubts about God's goodness or provision? Do we trust that our Father in heaven will provide our daily bread? Are we failing to forgive others as we have been forgiven? Prayer is the means we use to shoo the devil away!

CONTINUING THE DISCUSSION

1. "Our Father" is how Jesus tells us to address God. How does your relationship with your imperfect human father color that command? Does it draw you near to God or push you away?

2. Our ability to forgive others is perhaps our *greatest defense* against Satan's attempt to create footholds in our lives. Are there current relationships in which you are harboring an

unforgiving spirit or bitterness? What keeps you from approaching this person to address the issue? How might Satan be using your reluctance to establish a foothold?

3. Based on *status authority*, who are the specific people you have the power to intercede for on a regular basis (spouse, children, employees, students, etc.)? How does the reality of status authority motivate you to pray?

4. As a couple, take time to write your own warfare prayers. Which issue—world, flesh, or devil—seems most urgent? Commit to creating a draft of one prayer today. Remember, the first draft doesn't need to be perfect and can be modified over time.

7

TAKING THE DEVIL'S PERSPECTIVE

INSIGHTS FROM C. S. LEWIS

Would you walk in another person's shoes for one month?"
The challenge was given by producer Morgan Spurlock to a wide range of people, resulting in the hit FX series *30 Days*. In each episode participants agreed to place themselves in situations that challenged their perspective. Episodes included an atheist schoolteacher living with a conservative Christian family, a Christian attending a Muslim mosque, a person committed to deporting illegal immigrants picking oranges side by side with undocumented workers, a physically able person navigating a wheelchair in public places, a middle-class couple living on minimum wage, and so on. Thirty days spent seeing life through the eyes of another.

Long before Spurlock's hit show, Christian author C. S. Lewis created the ultimate perspective-taking project. Lewis sought to see the world not through the eyes of another person but through those of a demon. How does a demon seek to disrupt Christians? What tricks would he use to weaken people of faith? Does he work in concert with other demons? How does a demon learn his craft? What does communication between demons sound like as they strategize?

Lewis imaginatively submersed himself in their world not for merely thirty days but six months. The result was one of his most-read books, *The Screwtape Letters*. Lewis's book has been adapted into plays, converted into a comic book, and masterfully read as an audiobook by British comedic legend John Cleese. Five years after its release in 1942, Lewis was on the cover of *Time* magazine with a miniature devil on his shoulder. When asked what book helped him understand human nature, the late Supreme Court Justice Antonia Scalia referenced Lewis's book. Today, *The Screwtape Letters* is as relevant to followers of Christ as when it was first released. While Lewis's insights reflect his own thinking on issues, they prompt us to think creatively and deeply about spiritual realities rooted in church tradition and the Scriptures.

While *The Screwtape Letters* is filled with wide-ranging topics, what are the most important takeaways for couples desiring to learn more about demonic ways of tempting? Important concepts such as the principle of undulation, dangers of judging the intentions of others, gradual temptation, overly romantic view of love, selfishness, and ubiquitous noise are all explored.

INTRODUCTION TO SCREWTAPE LETTERS

Deeply disturbed by Adolf Hitler's ability to persuade others of his sinister vision, Lewis became intrigued with the idea of exploring how demons equally set out to influence and persuade. Originally titled *As One Devil to Another*, Lewis explores the personal letters from a senior devil, Screwtape, to a young devilish apprentice, Wormwood, who is tempting his very first human subject, referred to simply as "the patient." "The idea," writes Lewis to a friend, "would be to give all the psychology of temptation from the *other* point of view."[1]

Originally presented as a weekly column for a newspaper, readers were fascinated by getting an inside perspective on how temptation works. "My dear Wormwood" is how each of the thirty-one letters begins, and each closes with "Your affectionate uncle, Screwtape." All except the last letter, which ominously concludes with "Your increasingly and ravenously affectionate uncle." For those new to this imaginative dialogue, keep in mind that everything from a devil's perspective is inverted or reversed. Thus, the "Enemy" is God, and "Our Father Below" is a reference to the supreme commander, Satan. As couples seeking to cultivate Christ-honoring marriages, what can we learn from Screwtape's astute observations of us and the areas he seeks to exploit?

HUMANS LIVE COMFORTABLY WITH CONTRADICTORY BELIEFS

"Your man has been accustomed, ever since he was a little boy," writes Screwtape to his young protégé, "to have a dozen incompatible philosophies dancing about together inside his head."[2] Specifically, Screwtape is talking about the uneasy relationship many within the church have with the idea of Satan. Dancing about in our heads simultaneously is, on one hand, a belief that the Bible regularly speaks about spiritual warfare. Yet we also carry a belief that focusing on the devil is not worth our time. How can we believe Jesus took Satan seriously, yet as his followers fail to follow in his lead? Screwtape explains that judging our beliefs as right or wrong is replaced by asking if they are practical, outworn, or contemporary. The reality is that many of us find the thought of taking spiritual battle seriously as outdated and, if honest, embarrassing. We are not alone.

The upcoming generation of Christians is also leery of taking spiritual warfare seriously. When I ask my students to explain their hesitancy, I get responses like the following:

- I think talking about "Satan" and the "devil" are sort of buzzwords for a crazy person.

- Spiritual battle may not be talked about much because we don't want to recognize it as a reality.

- I think I avoid the topic because talking about it would make it real. And if it's real, then I have so many questions.

- Oddly, spiritual warfare has been normalized in culture through horror movies while being denied in the church. I know I've never heard my pastor preach on it.

- My pastor says that if I have God in my heart I don't need to worry about demons and spiritual attack. Is that true?

- I honestly can't remember the last time I had a conversation about spiritual warfare with my friends.

Notice that no argument has been offered by Screwtape as to *why* it is outdated or ignorant to believe in a personalized devil as described by the Scriptures. Screwtape closes his letter with a chilling insight into the tactics of demons: "Jargon, not argument, is your best ally."[3] Rather than arguing that belief in the devil is false or lacking evidence, simply label it as outdated. Screwtape's observation leaves us with a probing question: As couples, do we take our cues from Scripture or current cultural fads?

THE TRANSITION FROM THE IDEAL
TO THE REAL TAKES WORK

Demons are desperate to keep one pivotal truth hidden from us. Screwtape notes, "In every department of life," a difficult transition occurs, going from "dreaming aspirations to laborious doing."[4] In my martial arts school, we have many visitors. They have recently watched a Kung Fu movie on Netflix, ordered a UFC fight, or seen a Bruce Lee biopic, and think it would be cool to kick a person's head or learn to use a razor sharp double-edged sword. Predictably, most only last a week or two. Why? Moving from dreaming aspirations—breaking bricks with your hand—to thousands of hours of laborious practice is exhausting.

Screwtape specifically mentions how this difficult transition applies to marriage. "It occurs when lovers have gotten married and begin the real task of learning to live together."[5] One of today's leading relationship scholars, John Gottman, asserts that most of the arguing that occurs in a marriage happens in the first two years as the couple transitions from romantic courtship to establishing marital stability. He explains that the success of a marriage will depend on how the couple navigates three phases.[6] Phase one is identified as falling in love and is evidenced by fantasy, obsession, sexual attraction, and fear of rejection. Phase two requires couples to do the difficult work of building trust. *Can I count on you? Will you be there in difficult times? Are you merely concerned with your own interests?* Phase three entails establishing commitment and loyalty as evidenced by how the couple rates each other on the *fairness metric.* This crucial metric measure is how each spouse feels power is being distributed in the marriage. *Do I have a say in the direction of our marriage? Are my opinions heard? Is my vision for the marriage being equally considered?*

A key tactic of Screwtape is to get Christian couples to expect all the thrills and passion of phase one to equally carry over to other phases. Through poets and novelists, demons have successfully persuaded "humans that a curious, and usually short-lived, experience which they call 'being in love' is the only respectable grounds for marriage and that marriage can, and ought to, render this excitement permanent."[7] As a single, I'll never forget for the first time hearing a married friend announce, "Bro, marriage is work."

"What about passionate sex? Or the crazy love you exhibited while dating? You guys were inseparable!" I responded.

"We still are," he replied. "It's just that marriage isn't always this romantic high. At times," he paused, "it's just, well, putting in the effort whether you feel like it or not."

Now, having been married for over twenty-eight years I understand that marriage requires intentionality that helps couples through the transition from an overly romantic view of marriage to the hard work of making a relationship last.

In his book *Renovation of the Heart*, Dallas Willard argues that Christians need to address three components to help any aspiration succeed. He lays out these components in the acronym VIM:

Vision, Intention, Means. Willard explains VIM by having us consider a person who wants to learn a foreign language. This person surely will not succeed in learning a language unless she first has a vision for what it entails to learn one and how life will be changed once the skill is acquired. "Now, this is the *vision* that goes into the particular project of learning the language. Unless one has it—or, better, it has them—the language will pretty surely not be learned."[8]

Vision equally applies to our marriages. What is the vision for your marriage? In chapter two, taking our cue from the Union Rescue Mission, we considered how married Christians should seek to establish pockets of the kingdom within their neighborhood. In short, to model to others what a relationship looks like living out kingdom virtues. However, more is needed than mere vision.

Imagine a person desiring to learn a language sitting around waiting to see if the skill will, by chance, occur. Willard is quick to point out that vision without intention is meaningless. "We must intend the vision if it is to be realized. That is, we must initiate, bring into being those factors that would bring the vision to reality"[9] How a person intends to make a vision reality will necessarily include practical *means*. Imagine for a moment you were learning to speak Arabic. Willard notes that you "will sign up for language courses, listen to recordings, buy books, associate with people who speak Arabic, immerse yourself in the culture, possibly spend some intensive time in Jordan or Morocco, and practice, practice, practice."[10] Equally then, a couple wanting to be examples of kingdom living must also have means such as reading books about marriage, associating with like-minded couples, incorporating regular times of spiritual devotion, and practice, practice, practice. Screwtape's goal is for couples to have an overly romantic vision of love and marriage, and then to be deeply disillusioned by the *un*romantic laborious work it takes to flourish as a couple in the long term.

 Where did Hollywood scriptwriters and tempters like Screwtape get the idea that romantic love can totally fulfill us? In the mid-eighteenth century, poets, artists, and philosophers bought into the worldview of Romanticism, which still guides our modern notions of love. In part, key tenets are (1) passionate sex is the clearest measure of love; (2) the all-consuming and intoxicating feelings of young love can last for a lifetime; (3) the right partner can fully complete us and dispel all loneliness; (4) love can overcome social, economic, and religious differences; (5) choosing a life partner should be guided primarily by feelings, not practical considerations. Sound familiar?

JUDGING THE INTENTIONS OF OTHERS CAUSES PROBLEMS

"When two humans have lived together for many years it usually happens that each has tones of voice and expressions of face which are almost unendurably irritating to the other."[11] Over time, a spouse becomes convinced of the ability to infallibly read the intentions of a partner. Just by their actions, we know our spouse's intentions. *She went to bed early because she isn't interested in sex. He checks his cell phone when I'm talking because I bore him.* The trick, notes Screwtape, is to never let the person being tempted consider the possibility of being wrong. Judging another harshly is particularly linked to tone of voice. Screwtape writes, "In civilized life domestic hatred usually expresses itself by saying things which would appear quite harmless on paper (the *words* are not offensive) but in such a voice, or at such a moment, that they are not far short of a blow to the face."[12] Over time, a spouse becomes convinced he is getting *the look* from his wife, while she feels dismissed not by words but by *that tone*.

How can couples check their negative interpretations? To promote productive conversations we need to check the meanings we give to the actions of others through a process called *perception checking*. This crucial process has three distinct parts. First, provide a description of the behavior in question. Second, offer two possible interpretations of the behavior. Third, ask for clarification about how to interpret the behavior. For example, you ask your spouse if they are up for taking a walk, and they respond "Yeah, sure." You are immediately frustrated because you are *certain* the minimal response is a sign your spouse is not interested. We would feed into Screwtape's strategy by leaving our interpretation unchecked and allow anger toward our spouse to build. Try the following: "Tom, your answer didn't seem very enthusiastic. Are you a little tired, or just not up for it?" This gives Tom a chance to clarify his remark. "Sorry, I am a little tired, but would still like to walk." Remember, perception checking only works if your tone is appropriate and inviting.

LIFE IS A SERIES OF THREE STEPS FORWARD, TWO STEPS BACK

Having observed us for thousands of years, Screwtape understands a natural aspect of human life that he is eager to keep hidden.

Screwtape calls this natural flow *undulation*, which he describes as "the repeated return to a level from which they [humans] repeatedly fall back, a series of troughs and peaks."[13] In other words, life naturally fits into a series of highs and lows. We start a new job with enthusiasm, then periodically wrestle with waves of restlessness even if we value the work. "If you had watched your patient carefully," Screwtape prompts Wormwood, "you would have seen this undulation in every department of his life—his interest in his work, his affection for his friends, his physical appetites, all go up and down."[14]

Interestingly, the principle of undulation equally applies to our intimacy with God. "Sooner or later He [God] withdraws, if not in fact, at least from their conscious experience, all those supports and incentives." Why? "He leaves the creatures to stand up on its own legs—to carry out from the will alone duties which have lost all relish."[15]

The same applies to the best of marriages. If a couple has done the hard work of moving through Gottman's three phases and have established a solid foundation of trust and commitment, they *still* will experience natural peaks and troughs. Experiencing troughs does not mean anything is wrong with the marriage. The principle of undulation applies even to the most mature of Christian marriages. The contradictory nature of the low periods is that they offer both a unique time to honor God and a prime time for demonic temptation. When the relationship seems stale or filled with conflict, demons are quick to tempt us to think we have failed or the marriage is over. Many couples come up to me at marriage conferences deeply discouraged that even though they diligently work on their marriage, they still experience emotional valleys. "I hate to say it," one woman commented, "but sometimes my marriage is just plain vanilla. I grit my teeth and do the best I can." The mistake we make with the principle of undulation is to think the lows are permanent. Screwtape suggests that Wormwood make his patient believe that the trough or low time is the new normal. The lack of enthusiasm they have toward God or a spouse will never come back.

From God's perspective, during the troughs we most grow into the type of people God desires. "Hence the prayers offered in the state of dryness are those which please Him best."[16] God is most pleased when we decide, as a couple, to carry on in our marriage even when the thrill is temporarily gone and the work is hard. "The Enemy described a married couple as 'one flesh.' He did not say 'a happily married couple.'"[17] Our unity as a couple needs to be protected during regular times of dryness.

Even when we struggle, "He [God] is pleased even with their stumbles," Screwtape dejectedly notes.[18] These observations from Lewis—given to us via Screwtape—are deeply comforting as my wife and I go through troughs. Sometimes, during dry times with God or a spouse, we are left with only a desire to please God even though we limp along. However, the mere fact we desire to be faithful in low times brings pleasure to God. "I believe," notes Christian author Thomas Merton, "that the desire to please You does in fact please You."[19] Such resolute obedience during the lows of a marriage makes demons shudder.

READER   Can I ask you to clarify something?

AUTHOR   I haven't heard from you in a while. I was getting worried. What needs clarification?

READER   You seem to be suggesting that even in the best of
           Christian marriages there will be a certain amount
           of disappointment. Is that what you mean to say? If
           so, clarify.

AUTHOR   What I'm describing has been called "the argument
           from desire" by Christian philosophers.

READER   The argument from what?

AUTHOR   Desire. It's basically the idea that God—like elevator
           music—is always whispering in the background, in-
           viting us to look past our imperfect earthly pleasures
           toward him. While human love is good, we have been
           made for the perfect love of our heavenly Father. Thus,
           human love—no matter how pure—will always lack
           a little. The same with marriage.

READER   In an odd way, if I lower my expectations about love
           and marriage, I'll be more content. Is that right?

AUTHOR   Yes. When I no longer expect my spouse to love me
           perfectly—as only God can—I can become more
           content with imperfect human love. May I continue?

READER   By all means.

FRIENDS REALLY DO INFLUENCE
YOUR MARRIAGE

Screwtape informs Wormwood that he is delighted to learn that
"your patient has made some very desirable new acquaintances and
that you seem to have used this event in a really promising manner."[20]
Screwtape describes these new friends as superficially intellectual,
culturally religious, and "skeptical about everything in the world."[21]

He approvingly notes that the old warnings about a Christian's choice of friends is seldom written about by modern Christian authors. Screwtape acutely understands that no marriage exists on an island. The relationships around us deeply influence our marriage.

"Could your marriage be put at risk by a friend's divorce?" inquired researchers at the University of California, San Diego. The answer appears to be a firm yes. If your friend's marriage falls apart and ends up in divorce, your chance of divorcing increases by 75 percent. Even the breakup of a friend of a friend's marriage boosts your chances of divorce by a third. Social scientists call this phenomenon "divorce clustering" and compare it to a flu virus that spreads among friends and family. Lead researcher James H. Fowler observed that "people begin to warm up to the idea of divorce when they see their friends, family or co-workers going through the process. When a divorced person confides in someone married, the married person gains knowledge about the benefits and drawbacks of divorce."[22] Interestingly, Fowler noted that a majority of people in the study paid particular attention to the *benefits* in divorce (end of daily conflict, increased freedom, possibility of starting over) rather than the drawbacks or cost.

My wife and I experienced divorce clustering firsthand on our son's youth soccer team. Three families who were lifelong friends were shocked when one couple—the head coach—decided to divorce his wife. Soon after, the assistant coach and his wife separated. A year later, the third couple called it quits. In the span of one year, parents and young, impressionable players witnessed three divorces. Screwtape is right, those we associate with have potential to influence us and our relational bonds.

HUMANS ARE INHERENTLY SELFISH

The most reoccurring complaint from those attending marriage conferences where my wife and I speak is *my spouse is selfish*. This reality should not surprise us. The prophet Isaiah observed that "each of us has turned to our own way" (Is 53:6). As the demands of marriage—and possibly starting a family—grow, we become desperate to protect our time. Screwtape sees an opening for temptation here. He notes that interruptions from coworkers, spouse, or family infuriate the patient because "he regards his time as his own and feels that it is being stolen." Screwtape encourages Wormwood to fuel the unrealistic idea that he has the right to do as he wishes with his time. "Let him have the feeling that he starts each day as the lawful possessor of twenty-four hours."[23]

This desire to protect *my time* has been a regularly occurring struggle for me. I made the decision to pursue graduate school later in life, which thrust me into having to balance work, school, marriage, and a young family. Over time, as the demands of school mounted, I began to see *everything* as a speed bump to me getting things done! The difficulty was that while pushing through graduate school, I continued to speak at marriage conferences, where I had audiences consider Paul's admonition "Do nothing out of selfish ambition or vain conceit. Rather, in humility value others above yourselves." In case his point was missed, Paul continues, "not looking to your own interests but each of you to the interests of the others" (Phil 2:3-4). Notice that Paul affirms it is perfectly reasonable to focus on "your own interests." Yet that focus should not trump the "interests of the others." To illustrate, Paul appeals to the attitude adopted by Christ when he set aside self-interest and self-protection to secure our salvation (Phil 2:5-11). If anyone had a right to determine how to live out his days, it was the Son of God. Yet he regularly put the Father's agenda above his own. "Not my will, but yours," he prayed during a dark night in Gethsemane (Lk 22:42). Following Christ's lead will necessarily entail considering our spouse's needs in the midst of setting our own agenda.

Why no sequel? The popularity of Lewis's weekly columns and eventual book prompted readers to beg for more devilish letters. Lewis was simply not up for it. Putting himself into Screwtape's perspective meant entering a world where every "trace of beauty, freshness and geniality had to be excluded." He finally accepted an invitation from the *Saturday Evening Post*, and Screwtape's voice appeared one last time in the form of a toast delivered at the annual dinner of the Tempter's Training College for Young Devils held somewhere in the depths of hell. He begins, "Mr. Principal, your Imminence, your Disgraces."*

*C. S. Lewis, *Screwtape Proposes a Toast* (Bel Air, CA: Fount Publishers, 1993).

HUMANS LOVE DISTRACTION

In one of his letters, Screwtape provides a fascinating insight into what most annoys demons—silence. The goal of the Father Below is to fill every inch of the universe with mind-numbing noise. "We will make the whole universe a noise in the end." Why is noise so desirable? "Noise which alone defends us from silly qualms, despairing scruples and impossible desires." Screwtape then chillingly observes, "We have already made great strides in this direction as regards the Earth."[24]

The need for silence that fuels solitude and mindfulness is seen in both the Scriptures and marital research. Many who study the spiritual disciplines argue that the practice of solitude is the fundamental discipline. It is the decision to voluntarily abstain from speaking or exposing ourselves to outside noise or stimulus in order to open ourselves to Spirit-led introspection. "Search me, God," declares David, "and know my heart; test me and know my anxious thoughts" (Ps 139:23). Christian thinker Blaise Pascal once commented that if he could prescribe one thing for an ailing society, it would be for each of us to sit alone in a room in quiet contemplation.[25] The difficulty is that in today's techno-savvy world we have developed an aversion to silence. When we do sit alone in a room, technological distractions are plentiful. Add to this, many of us simply have no idea how to invite silence into our hectic schedules.

In our fast-paced, media-saturated world, spending a day or afternoon in silence is difficult. However, could we seek to create pockets of solitude throughout the day? Instead of jumping out of bed to join the rush, spend a few minutes asking God to direct your thoughts about your relationships. Before you turn on the computer or check text messages, take a minute or two to be silent. Turn off the radio during your commute to work or class, and tune into God's perspective.[26]

A loss of solitude is not the only casualty of our media-obsessed noisy world. Marital research has uncovered a type of communication noise fostered by technology that seemingly interferes with relational connection that is called *technoference*. Researchers at Brigham Young University coined the term after studying the negative effects of technology on relationships. In their study, 114 married or cohabitating women reported that phones, computers, and other technological devices inhibited intimacy. These participants reported increased loss of mindfulness and sense of connection, and higher levels of conflict. The main culprit? Interference caused by a cell phone seems to be particularly disruptive and hurtful. "When your partner attends to a phone instead of to you, it feels like rejection—it *hurts*. Feeling ignored when your partner is on their phone can feel as bad as being shunned."[27]

The key to eliminating technoference is, in part, to govern technology use in a marriage. *Constitutive rules* are created by a couple to identify what counts as what in a relationship. What counts as mindfulness or attentiveness during a conversation? What counts as an acceptable reason to check a cell phone while in the midst of a conversation? What level of environmental silence is needed to fully engage each other? In a demon's vision for our world, noise would fill every corner of our lives and relationships. Resisting this demonic vision will entail creating pockets of solitude void of technoference that keeps us from hearing God's voice and the voice of our spouse.

LEARNING FROM LEWIS

The creative observations of Lewis have greatly helped my wife and me understand and prepare for spiritual battle in our marriage. The observations we've just considered have challenged us to think deeply about the subtleness of spiritual opposition. I concur with Christian authors Jamin Goggin and Kyle Strobel, who assert that demonic powers often "work beneath the radar" and are so "subtle and ingrained in the fabric of our culture that we don't even recognize their presence."[28] Here are the observations of Lewis that particularly have helped us as a couple.

Humans love distraction. Screwtape informs us that Satan's goal is to fill the universe with mind-numbing noise that distracts us from each other and God. Culture watcher Nancy Sleeth seems to suggest that technoference is widespread and damaging to relationships. "People tell me they could not live without their cell phones or the internet or e-mail—and they mean it. Yet in many ways, these technologies lead us to more disconnected—rather than connected—lives."[29] As a couple, my wife and I resonate with Sleeth's observation. For us, the greatest culprit responsible for creating techonoference is surfing social media on our laptop computers. Slowly, Noreen and I got into the habit of checking emails as soon as we got out of bed in the morning, which in turn pulls us into a technological riptide. At night, we'd sit with laptops open as we try to share what happened that day. Or at the end of the day we'd relax and watch a favorite show with laptops open trying to multitask. Over time, we became concerned that technology was curtailing our ability to be fully present with each other. Slowly, our communication was filled with the ubiquitous noise described by Screwtape.

What to do? To counteract technoference we decided to periodically engage in a technology fast. The fast consisted of setting aside three days in which we would take a break from the form of technology that was most distracting. In our case, it was clearly our laptops. Unless it was work related and *urgent*, we resisted the urge to start the day by checking emails or the latest breaking news updates. The first part of the morning was spent tech free as we discussed the upcoming day. After breakfast, we were free to check emails to see if any needed an immediate response before heading into work. In the evening, we decided to take a walk or watch a show with laptops or cell phones off. This three-day tech fast was both diagnostic (how much did we miss technology) and useful in developing a discipline where we controlled media intake.

During the fast we consider what technology means to us as a couple. What are the benefits of technology? How does it help us stay connected with each other or our kids? Alternatively, how has it contributed to negative feelings like isolation, anxiety, or fear of missing out? When we feel technoference raise its addictive head, we engage in a tech fast. Removing technological noise helps us not only connect on an interpersonal level but gives us perspective how the evil one may be using *noise* to hinder our intimacy.

Friends influence your marriage. Screwtape's observation that modern Christian authors seldom talk about the value of wisely choosing friends is troubling. To know our marriage could be put at risk by the divorce of those around us makes us eager to surround ourselves with people who value marriage and take spiritual opposition seriously. While learning of divorce clustering is sobering, we must keep in mind a key observation. While it seems the actions of our friends can negatively impact us, the inverse is equally true. Associating with friends who regularly affirm their marriage vows, speak highly of each other, and seek to center their marriage on Christ will no doubt positively influence your marriage. While no Christian couple should isolate themselves from those experiencing marital crisis, we also need to develop a support group of like-minded believers who hold a similar view of marriage.

What to do? When Noreen and I moved coast to coast so I could teach at Biola University, our highest priority was to be on the lookout for couples who would be interested in forming a marriage group. One of the favorite strategies of the evil one is to isolate couples and entice them to believe that the marital or parental struggles they are experiencing are unique to them. To hear that another couple struggles with the exact issue you do is liberating and solidifies your marital bond. As the ancient writer reminds us, isolated people can easily be overcome, while "a cord of three strands is not quickly broken" (Eccles 4:12).

Humans are inherently selfish. As Christians, we are pulled in two directions. Our selfish nature tempts us to fixate on and protect our own needs, while the Scriptures call us to give preference to the needs of others (Phil 2:3-4). As we've already considered, following Christ entails our consistently putting the needs of our spouse ahead of our desires or wants. The pull toward selfishness or selflessness is most acutely felt in the area of sexual intimacy. No doubt devilish tempters delight in using sex as a means of fostering hurt, selfishness, and disappointment. Here are some ways I've seen couples struggle with this most intimate form of human connection.

First, our physical differences open the door for potential self-centeredness. Roughly, men need merely two or three minutes of stimulation to achieve orgasm, while women "generally need ten times that amount of time."[30] The differences don't stop there. Most men easily achieve orgasm during intercourse, while a majority of women can't achieve orgasm without direct and prolonged stimulation of their clitoris. During a man's orgasm his body releases a hormone called oxytocin, which makes him want to sleep after sex.[31] Do you see where selfishness can easily come into play? While being intimate, a man achieves orgasm quickly and then wants to sleep. Conversely, his wife needs much more time to achieve pleasure. In fact, on average fifteen minutes more time and attention.

How will a husband respond to this physiological difference? There's little doubt that tempters such as Screwtape would want to exploit these differences, resulting in a husband—flooded with oxytocin—growing increasingly impatient with a wife's slow response. Does he fight off sleepiness and physical fatigue to patiently love his wife or merely kiss her on the forehead and go to sleep? Surprisingly, sexual intimacy can become fertile ground for developing the discipline of selflessness. Keep lines of communication open. Take time to understand the physical differences that cause men and women to respond to sexual stimulation in different ways—responses often outside of our control.

For men, a key physical response to achieving an orgasm is physical tiredness via hormones being released in his body. For a woman, the slowness of an orgasm is frustrating for her and often results in her forgoing an orgasm—or pretending it happens—in order to not frustrate her spouse. Empathy is the ability to see the world through the eyes of another. Openly talking about our sexual differences not only can produce understanding between spouses but offer protection from the temptation to be selfish.

Second, when starting their marriage couples often think that sex will come naturally. When Noreen and I do premarital counseling with couples, we dispel the idea that when two Christians get married the sex will be natural and immediately pleasurable. Our experience with couples tells us that sex is often confusing.

One young couple, who had set strong sexual boundaries while
dating, seemed dejected when we asked how sex was going during
our six-month follow-up after the wedding. "Can I be honest?" responded the wife. "Sex isn't what I thought it would be. It's been
mostly frustrating." They explained that discovering what is and
isn't pleasurable has caused friction between them. He explained
that it's been awkward to talk about sex, so it mostly has been trial
and error followed by feelings of inadequacy. "The last thing I want
to do is make my wife feel like I'm judging her lovemaking abil-
ities," he confessed.

What to do? We shared with this young couple that it might be
good to create a sexual road map for each other. A sexual road map
is an idea Noreen and I came across years ago. Separately, a couple
writes out in detail how they would like a night of lovemaking to
proceed each step of the way. A road map could begin by asking for
a back massage, followed by cuddling, tender kissing, and so on.
The map provides crucial information on what *is* and *is not* pleasurable. The map only works if each suggestion can be honestly
discussed and perhaps declined or modified. For many couples,
writing what is pleasurable or desirable and having a spouse read
it takes away some of the awkwardness.

When discussing the road map, a common question is, For
Christians, what forms of sex are off-limits? Our general answer is
that several criteria should be used. First, is the form of sexual
intimacy being considered *mutually* pleasurable? It's crucial that a
spouse feel the freedom to decline any form of sexual intimacy that
makes them feel uncomfortable. Second, at no time should a
spouse feel pressured into a particular form of sexual intimacy.

Last, the proposed act must be *safe*. Before any sexual act is suggested or attempted, research must be done on potential health risks. To engage in any form of sexual intimacy that is potentially dangerous or degrading must be discarded.

Screwtape's last letter is full of resignation and simmering anger as the patient has not only become a Christian but has died and now stands in the enemy's (God's) loving presence. While he is in the midst of such grace and acceptance, it is no longer possible to tempt him. In that moment, the patient saw "Him" and "the central music in every pure experience which had always just evaded memory was now at last recovered."[32] In that final meeting, like a traveler stripping off old clothes, the patient was finally in God's presence and beyond *all* tempting.

CONTINUING THE CONVERSATION

1. Dallas Willard explains that for change to occur we must have vision, intention, and means. What is the overall *vision* for your marriage? How committed are you to making that vision a reality (intention)? What *means* (reading books, starting a marriage group, attending a marriage conference, marriage counseling) will help you achieve your vision?

2. How often do you engage in perception checking with your spouse? How regularly do you consider two or more interpretations of a spouse's actions? Or do you merely lock in on one negative judgment?

3. In light of divorce clustering, make a list of couples whose breakup would have a deep impact on you. What is it about their marriages that you admire? If a couple you admired

were experiencing deep struggles, what steps would you take to help?

4. What forms of technoference consistently interfere with your ability to connect as a couple? Is there one form of technology your partner engages in that makes you particularly feel shunned or ignored?

CONCLUSION

Nine minutes into the game and I start to feel tense.

The Soviet Union has scored and the upstart American hockey team is bracing for the goal onslaught that is sure to come. The fears of the American players are warranted in light of their most recent encounter with the Soviet juggernaut. Two weeks before the 1980 Winter Olympics in Lake Placid, New York, the teams squared off in an exhibition game at Madison Square Garden. The Soviets—defending gold medalists made up of seasoned professionals—crushed the young, inexperienced American team 10-3. Now, with the score of a quick goal in the Olympic rematch, it seemed a massacre was certain. I uncomfortably shift in my chair in front of the television.

Along with my wife, I'm rewatching my favorite sports movie, *Miracle* (2004) which retells one of the most famous hockey games ever played now dubbed the "Miracle on Ice." Shockingly, at the end of the first period the Americans have somehow weathered the first storm and the game is tied 2-2. My heart sinks again when the

Soviets score quickly to start the second period. It's at this point in the movie that my wife takes my hand. "Remember, we win," she says with a smile.

In one of the greatest sports upsets ever, the Americans win the Olympic contest with the Soviets 4-3. The game concludes with ABC sports announcer Al Michaels famously shouting, "Do you believe in miracles?" Americans do believe, and the US team goes on to win gold.

My wife's words serve as a much-needed reminder to Christian couples as we experience the ups and downs of spiritual battle. As we seek to live out biblical convictions as a couple, there will be times when it seems demonic forces are getting the best of us. There will be days, perhaps even long seasons of a marriage, when it seems that we've allowed spiritual footholds—bitterness, unresolved conflict, not believing the best about your spouse, lack of forgiveness, hopelessness—to take root. Seemingly, Satan is on the verge of victory in our relationships. At these moments, we must remember what the Scriptures say about the outcome of our struggle.

While the topic of Satan's final demise is complex and cannot be covered fully here, one aspect is perfectly clear—with Christ's final return his enemies will be stripped of power. Paul confidently asserts that when Christ comes he will destroy *all* demonic opposition, resulting in his enemies being put "under his feet" (1 Cor 15:24-25). Clint Arnold states that from Paul's perspective Satan and his reign of terror "face a definite point in history when their tyranny will be brought to an end." However, today they function like a pack of wild dogs on long leashes. "When Christ returns, he will tighten the leash to such an extent that they will not be able to cause any harm or instill any fear whatsoever. They will be completely pacified."[1]

In the meantime, how should Christian couples respond? Should we hunker down and ride out the demonic storm until Jesus comes back? Or should we seek to reclaim enemy-held territory? We have been given the privilege of offering release to those whose lives have been deeply wounded and scarred by a culture molded by evil forces. If we reject the idea that our marriages are merely in a holding pattern until Jesus returns, or a means to secure some form of the American Dream, how then should we act? What if we took seriously the idea that our marriages are outposts of God's kingdom? Each of us—individually and as couples—are Christ's ambassadors through whom God makes his appeal to a world desperate for the touch of divine love (2 Cor 5:20). If we embrace this calling, shouldn't we assume that the evil one is powerful and presently at work to derail us?

Certainly not all marital struggles are demon induced, but is it wise to assume the evil one is probing defenses, seeking to establish a foothold? Does the Bible suggest we ignore the threat, or are we to acknowledge the reality of a spiritual foe targeting our marriage? We can be assured that the days ahead will be filled with wisely discerning whether spiritual attack is happening, adorning ourselves in spiritual protection, crafting spiritual warfare prayers, and claiming our Christ-given authority. Spiritual opposition did not start because you read a book about it. Rather, it has been happening all around us since the first temptation in a garden environment. Now that we are aware of the struggle, it's time to stand firm and respond as a couple.

We can be assured that using biblical weapons and strategies will ensure regular victories, helping our marriages to grow and even flourish. Conversely, there will be anxious moments when spiritual attack feels unrelenting. In those moments, reach for your spouse's hand and whisper, "Remember, we win."

ACKNOWLEDGMENTS

Writing a book is always a collaborative effort that upon completion requires many notes of appreciation.

Al Hsu, over the years you have been an amazingly insightful and caring editor—this book greatly benefited from your keen suggestions and guidance. Thank you.

Clint Arnold, you are one of the most insightful and generous scholars I've had the pleasure of meeting. I fondly remember our many coffee meetings where you patiently answered my questions about spiritual battle. Your insight and scholarly fingerprints are throughout this book. I am blessed to have you as a colleague.

Thank you to our marriage group—Jon and Pam, Rick and Shari, Doug and Deb, Dave and Debbie, Greg and Jeannie, Chris and Alisa—for your insight and encouragement. Doug Huffman, I'm especially indebted to your friendship and scholarly and editorial touch.

A special shout out goes to Kay Vinci for enthusiastically and tirelessly reading early drafts and giving keen input.

Many of these chapters were written or outlined during a month sharing study carrels and resources with fellows at the Tyndale House in Cambridge, England. Thanks for the lively conversations and timely breaks for tea.

Dennis Rainey, I am so appreciative of you allowing me to be part of the FamilyLife speaker team all these years and gradually formulating my thoughts on marriage and spiritual battle. You are so generous in sharing your platform with others.

Bill, for the majority of my life you've provided laughter, friendship, and insight—including on this manuscript.

Last, thank you to my wife, Noreen, who for over twenty-eight years has been through many spiritual battles with me—thanks for marching forward shoulder to shoulder.

INTRODUCTION

[1]Clinton Arnold, *Powers of Darkness: Principalities and Powers in Paul's Letters* (Downers Grove, IL: InterVarsity Press, 1992), 148.

[2]Arnold, *Powers of Darkness*, 16.

[3]C. S. Lewis, *The Screwtape Letters* (New York: HarperCollins, 1982), ix.

1 THE FIRST STEP

[1]Kenneth Boa, *Conformed to His Image: Biblical and Practical Approaches to Spiritual Formation* (Grand Rapids: Zondervan, 2001), 348.

[2]For more information on how the global Christian community approaches spiritual battle see Mary Anne Voelkel and Jack Voelkel, *Spiritual Warfare in Mission* (Downers Grove, IL: InterVarsity Press, 2012).

[3]Rudolf Bultmann, *New Testament and Mythology, and Other Basic Writings*, ed. and trans. Schubert M. Ogden (Philadelphia: Fortress, 1984), 4.

[4]Hans Küng, *On Being a Christian* (Garden City, NY: Doubleday, 1976), 369.

[5]Howard Munro, "Are Demons Real?," *St. Mark's Review* 145 (Autumn 1991): 38.

[6]Helmut Thielicke, *The Prayer That Spans the World: Sermons on the Lord's Prayer* (London: James Clarke, 1965), 160.

[7]Paul Enns, *The Moody Handbook of Theology* (Chicago: Moody Press, 1989), 292.

[8]Enns, *Moody Handbook of Theology*, 292.

[9]Millard J. Erickson, *Christian Theology*, 2nd ed. (Grand Rapids: Baker Academic, 1998), 472.

[10]Jewish expositors, as well as early church fathers, have traditionally assumed Satan was being addressed in both passages. Theologian Wayne Grudem, who supports this view, notes that it "would not be uncommon for Hebrew prophetic speech to pass from descriptions of human events to descriptions of heavenly events that are parallel to them and that the earthly events picture in a limited way" (Wayne Grudem, *Systematic Theology: An Introduction to Biblical Doctrine* [Grand Rapids: Zondervan, 1994], 413). While this is the traditional view, others have offered alternative perspectives about the fall of Satan. See, for example, B. J. Oropeza, *99 Answers to Questions About Angels, Demons and Spiritual Warfare* (Downers Grove, IL: InterVarsity Press, 1997), 70-88.

[11]Enns, *Moody Handbook of Theology*, 294.

[12]Merril F. Unger, *Demons in the World Today* (Wheaton, IL: Tyndale House, 1971), 16.

[13]The provocative topic of possible demon possession of a follower of Christ will be the subject of future chapters.

[14]The idea of incorporating an imaginary reader was inspired by the creative writings of Christian philosopher Peter Kreeft. Imitation, as they say, is the greatest form of flattery.

[15]John Ortberg, "Fighting the Good Fight: What Does the Bible Mean by 'Spiritual Warfare'?," *Leadership Journal*, Spring 2012, 25.

2 WHY WOULD SATAN CARE ABOUT MY MARRIAGE?

[1]Gerald H. Wilson, *Psalms*, NIV Application Commentary (Grand Rapids: Zondervan, 2002), 1:205.

[2]Some theologians argue that this Hebrew phrase could be interpreted "a little higher than angels." If so, imagine how much more irked Satan would be knowing he was under human beings?

[3]C. S. Lewis, *The Screwtape Letters* (New York: HarperCollins, 1982), 174.

[4]Lewis, *Screwtape Letters*, 208.

[5]Clint Arnold, *Powers of Darkness: Principalities and Powers in Paul's Letters* (Downers Grove, IL: InterVarsity Press, 1992), 81.

[6]Richard Lints, *The Fabric of Theology: A Prolegomenon to Evangelical Theology* (Grand Rapids: Eerdmans, 1993), 104.

[7]Bob Larkin, "What Escorts Can Teach a Married Man," *Men's Health*, November 2016, 99.

[8]David Popenoe, "Can the Nuclear Family Be Revived?," *Society*, July–August 1999, www .csub.edu/~rdugan2/can%20the%20nuclear%20family%20be%20revived.pdf.

[9]Clifford Nass, quoted in Drake Baer, "What Multitasking Does to Your Brain," *Leadership Now*, October 9, 2013, www.fastcompany.com/3019659/what-multitasking-does-to-your -brain.

[10]Nass, quoted in Baer, "What Multitasking Does to Your Brain."

[11]Guy Winch, "10 Real Risks of Multitasking, to Mind and Body," *Psychology Today*, June 22, 2016, www.psychologytoday.com/blog/the-squeaky-wheel /201606/10-real-risks -multitasking-mind-and-body.

[12]Aaron Smith and Monica Anderson, "5 Facts About Online Dating," Pew Research Center, February 20, 2016, www.pewresearch.org/fact-tank/2016 /02/29/5-facts-about -online-dating.

[13]Eben Harrell, "Are Romantic Movies Bad for You?," *Time*, December 23, 2008, http:// content.time.com/time/health/article/0,8599,1868389,00.html.

[14]"At Night on Skid Row, Nearly 2,000 Homeless People Share Just Nine Toilets," *Guardian*, June 2017, www.theguardian.com/us-news/2017/jun/30/la-skid-row-homeless-toilet -access-report.

[15]Tim Muehlhoff and Rick Langer, *Winsome Persuasion: Christian Influence in a Post-Christian World* (Downers Grove, IL: IVP Academic, 2017), 46.

[16]Walter Brueggemann, *Sabbath as Resistance: Saying No to the Culture of Now* (Louisville, KY: Westminster John Knox Press, 2014), 85.

[17]Augustine, *Confessions*, bk. I, chap. 1, trans. Rex Warner (New York: Mentor, 1963), p. 4.

[18]A. Skevington Wood, "Ephesians," in *The Expositor's Bible Commentary*, ed. Frank E. Gaebelein (Grand Rapids: Zondervan, 1978), 76.

[19]To learn more about what the Puritans can teach us, see Joanne's book *Godly Conversation: Rediscovering the Puritan Practice of Conference* (Grand Rapids: Reformation Heritage Books, 2011).

[20]Arnold, *Powers of Darkness*, 148.

3 HOW CAN I TELL IF THIS IS SPIRITUAL WARFARE?

[1]"State Office Takes over Penn State Fraternity Death Case," NBC10, January 8, 2018, www .nbcphiladelphia.com/news/local/Penn-State-Fraternity-Death-State-Office-Takeover -Student-Hazing-468367763.html.

[2]Clint Arnold, *Powers of Darkness: Principalities and Powers in Paul's Letters* (Downers Grove, IL: InterVarsity Press, 1992), 128.

[3]Arnold, *Powers of Darkness*, 129.

[4]Keith Ferdinando, *The Message of Spiritual Warfare* (Downers Grove, IL: InterVarsity Press, 2016), 194.

[5]Kenneth Boa, *Conformed to His Image: Biblical and Practical Approaches to Spiritual Formation* (Grand Rapids: Zondervan, 2001), 345.

[6]Clint Arnold, personal correspondence with the author, February 20, 2017.

[7]Martin Luther, *Table Talk* 4, 5097, cited by Louis Coulange, *The Life of the Devil* (London: Alfred A. Knopf, 1929), 147-48.

[8]Ancient philosophers identify anger as the "moral emotion" since it often propels us to address injustices or engage in peacemaking.

[9]While spousal battery can happen to men, the majority of violence is directed at women. See Julia Wood, *Gendered Lives: Communication, Gender, and Culture*, 10th ed. (Boston: Wadsworth, 2012).

[10]Curt Thompson, *The Soul of Shame: Retelling the Stories We Believe About Ourselves* (Downers Grove, IL: InterVarsity Press, 2015), 63.

[11]Thompson, *Soul of Shame*, 63.

[12]Dietrich Bonhoeffer, *Life Together* (New York: HarperCollins, 1954), 112.

[13]My thoughts about the complexity of love were first explored in Tim Muehlhoff, "Before You Pop the Question: Five Keys to a Love That Lasts." *Discipleship Journal* 166 (2008): 34-39.

[14]Naomi Wolf, "The Porn Myth," *New York*, 2017, http://nymag.com/nymetro/news/trends /n_9437.

[15]Nancy Tartaglone, "Fifty Shades Freed Collars $97M Overseas," Yahoo Entertainment, February 13, 2018, www.yahoo.com/entertainment/fifty-shades-freed-collars-98m -181625251.html.

[16]Wolf, "Porn Myth."

[17]Clint Arnold notes, "A believer may yield to the evil impulse or to a demonic spirit, allowing it to assert a dominating influence over mind, will, emotions, and even the body. But the person's new identity as a child of God cannot be erased or stolen." Clint Arnold, *Three Crucial Questions About Spiritual Warfare* (Grand Rapids: Baker Academic, 1997), 85.

4 THE SERPENT WAS CRAFTY

[1]Bevin Alexander, *How Great Generals Win* (New York: Norton, 1993), 22.

[2]J. Oswald Sanders, *Satan Is No Myth* (Eugene, OR: Wipf & Stock, 1975), 43.

[3]D. G. Kehl, "Sneaky Stimuli and How to Resist Them," *Christianity Today*, January 31, 1975, 30.

[4]Derek Kidner, *Genesis: An Introduction and Commentary* (Downers Grove, IL: Inter-Varsity Press, 1967), 66.

[5]"The Bible in America: 6-Year Trends," Barna Research Group, June 15, 2016, www.barna.com/research/the-bible-in-america-6-year-trends.

[6]Wendell Berry, "The Peace of Wild Things," *On Being* (blog), December 8, 2016, https://onbeing.org/blog/wendell-berry-the-peace-of-wild-things.

[7]To read more of this argument, see John H. Walton, *Genesis*, NIV Application Commentary (Grand Rapids: Zondervan, 2001), 170-72.

[8]Walton, *Genesis*, 206.

[9]For further understanding of communication concepts such as latent conflict, cross-complaining, and kitchen-sinking, consult Julia Wood, *Interpersonal Communication: Everyday Encounters*, 7th ed. (Belmont, CA: Wadsworth, 2012).

[10]Annalee Newitz, "Why Americans Became Obsessed with Ninjas," *io9*, February 6, 2014, http://io9.gizmodo.com/5982187/why-americans-became-obsessed-with-ninjas.

5 FIGHTING BACK AS A COUPLE

[1]Keith Ferdinando, *The Message of Spiritual Warfare* (Downers Grove, IL: InterVarsity Press, 2016), 249.

[2]Kenneth S. Wuest, *Wuest's Word Studies from the Greek New Testament* (Grand Rapids: Eerdmans, 1959), 1:141.

[3]Wuest, *Wuest's Word Studies*, 1:141.

[4]Ferdinando, *Message of Spiritual Warfare*, 252.

[5]Ferdinando, *Message of Spiritual Warfare*, 253.

[6]In my school, when you earn a black belt no protection is used in sparring. Without pads there is no false sense of security—miss a punch and you get hit. Period.

[7]Donald S. Whitney, *Spiritual Disciplines for the Christian Life* (Colorado Springs, CO: NavPress, 1997), 21.

[8]Clinton E. Arnold, *Ephesians*, Zondervan Exegetical Commentary on the New Testament (Grand Rapids: Zondervan, 2010), 444.

[9]"Umass Amherst Researcher Finds Most People Lie in Everyday Conversations," UMass-Amherst, January 10, 2002, www.umass.edu/newsoffice/article/umass-amherst-researcher-finds-most-people-lie-everyday-conversation.

[10]Jeff Nilsson, "Are Americans Less Truthful Today?," *Saturday Evening Post*, December 1, 2016, www.saturdayeveningpost.com/2016/12/01/history/post-perspective/convincing-truth-post-truth-politics.html.

[11]J. Oswald Sanders, *Satan Is No Myth* (Eugene, OR: Wipf & Stock, 1975), 94.

[12]Wuest, *Wuest's Word Studies*, 143.

[13]Tim Muehlhoff, *Marriage Forecasting: Changing the Climate of Your Relationship One Conversation at a Time* (Downers Grove, IL: InterVarsity Press, 2010), 60.

[14]Howard Hendricks, personal correspondence with the author, January 16, 1998. While most likely not original to "Prof"—as friends call him—his words have stayed with me.

[15]Wuest, *Wuest's Word Studies*, 41.

[16]Even though our footing with God is firm, our sinful actions may produce consequences that deeply affect not only ourselves but those we love. As Paul powerfully notes, we often reap what we sow (Gal 6:7).

[17]I'm indebted to my friend Jane Armstrong for passing along this illustration.

[18]Michael Lipka, "Why America's 'Nones' Left Religion Behind," Pew Research Center, August 24, 2016, www.pewresearch.org/fact-tank/2016/08/24/why-americas-nones-left-religion-behind/.

[19]While there are many insightful books that help Christians tackle difficult questions about faith, I suggest you start with J. P. Moreland and Tim Muehlhoff, *The God Conversation: Using Illustrations and Stories to Explain Your Faith*, exp. ed. (Downers Grove, IL: InterVarsity Press, 2017).

[20]Ronald E. Heine, *Commentaries of Origen and Jerome on St. Paul's Epistle to the Ephesians* (Oxford: Oxford Publications, 2002), 256-65.

[21]Jeremy Weber, "80% of Churchgoers Don't Read Bible Daily, Lifeway Survey Suggests," *Christianity Today*, September 7, 2012, www.christianitytoday.com/news/2012/september/80-of-churchgoers-dont-read-bible-daily-lifeway-survey.html.

6 OUR GREATEST DEFENSE: PRAYER

[1]Kenneth Boa, *Conformed to His Image: Biblical and Practical Approaches to Spiritual Formation* (Grand Rapids: Zondervan, 2001), 354.

[2]Many biblical scholars question whether the final phrase, "For yours is the kingdom and the power and the glory forever," was in the original Greek New Testament. Some speculate that it was added by early church leaders to formally close out the prayer. See R. T. Kendall, *The Sermon on the Mount: A Verse-by-Verse Look at the Greatest Teachings of Jesus* (Grand Rapids: Monarch Books, 2011), 263-68.

[3]John Stott, *The Message of the Sermon on the Mount* (Downers Grove, IL: InterVarsity Press, 1978), 148.

[4]Neil T. Anderson, *The Bondage Breaker* (Eugene, OR: Harvest House, 2000), 151.

[5]Stott, *Message of the Sermon on the Mount*, 146.

[6]Stott, *Message of the Sermon on the Mount*, 146.

[7]Kendall, *Sermon on the Mount*, 227.

[8]Michael J. Wilkins, *Matthew*, NIV Application Commentary (Grand Rapids: Zondervan, 2004), 277.

[9]Dallas Willard, *Renovation of the Heart: Putting on the Character of Christ* (Colorado Springs, CO: NavPress, 2002), 86.

[10]Kendall, *Sermon on the Mount*, 239.

[11]Kendall, *Sermon on the Mount*, 240.

[12]Kendall, *Sermon on the Mount*, 241.

[13]While it's debated if Getty used those exact words, we do know he was extremely pro-tective of his wealth, even going so far as to install a pay phone in his mansion for guests to use. Eventually, Getty paid $2.2 million of the ransom demand (maximum amount of money that was tax deductible). For more about Getty see Mike Miller and Nina Biddle, "A Billion-Dollar Heir and a Sliced-Off Ear: The Brutal True Story of J. Paul Getty III's Kidnapping," *People*, December 25, 2017, http://people.com/movies/true-story-all-money-world-j-paul-getty-iii-kidnapping.

[14]Michael Wilkins, *Matthew*, NIV Application Commentary (Grand Rapids: Zondervan, 2002), 279.

[15]This view is powerfully articulated by Charles Kraft, "Cleaning House: An Interview with Charles Kraft," *Leadership Journal*, Spring 2002, 42.

[16]John Ortberg, "Fighting the Good Fight: What Does the Bible Mean by 'Spiritual Warfare?,'" *Leadership Journal*, Spring 2002, 26.

[17]Joachim Jeremias, *New Testament Theology: The Proclamation of Jesus* (New York: Scrib-ner's, 1971), 202.

[18]Charles H. Kraft, *I Give You Authority: Practicing the Authority Jesus Gave Us* (Grand Rapids: Baker, 1997), 35.

[19]Kraft, *I Give You Authority*, 35.

[20]Kraft, *I Give You Authority*, 45.

[21]Kraft, *I Give You Authority*, 85.

[22]Kraft, *I Give You Authority*, 87.

[23]Kraft, *I Give You Authority*, 87.

[24]To read the full prayer, see Kenneth Boa: *Conformed to His Image: Biblical and Practical Approaches to Spiritual Formation* (Grand Rapids: Zondervan, 2001), 356.

7 TAKING THE DEVIL'S PERSPECTIVE

[1]Walter Hooper, *C. S. Lewis: Companion and Guide* (New York: HarperCollins, 1996), 267.

[2]C. S. Lewis, *The Screwtape Letters* (New York: HarperCollins, 1982), 1.

[3]Lewis, *Screwtape Letters*, 1.

[4]Lewis, *Screwtape Letters*, 7.

[5]Lewis, *Screwtape Letters*, 7.

[6]John Gottman, "The 3 Phases of Love," Gottman Institute, November 19, 2014, www.gottman.com/blog/the-3-phases-of-love.

[7]Lewis, *Screwtape Letters*, 93.

[8]Dallas Willard, *Renovation of the Heart: Putting on the Character of Christ* (Colorado Springs, CO: NavPress, 2002), 83. For a fuller discussion of VIM see my book *I Beg to Differ: Navigating Difficult Conversations in Truth and Love* (Downers Grove, IL: Inter-Varsity Press, 2015).

[9]Willard, *Renovation of the Heart*, 84.

[10]Willard, *Renovation of the Heart*, 84.

[11]Lewis, *Screwtape Letters*, 13.

[12]Lewis, *Screwtape Letters*, 13.

[13]Lewis, *Screwtape Letters*, 37.

[14]Lewis, *Screwtape Letters*, 37.

[15]Lewis, *Screwtape Letters*, 40.

[16]Lewis, *Screwtape Letters*, 40.

[17]Lewis, *Screwtape Letters*, 95.

[18]Lewis, *Screwtape Letters*, 95.

[19]Thomas Merton, quoted in Trent T. Gilliss, "Thomas Merton's Prayer That Anyone Can Pray," *On Being* (blog), December 28, 2014, https://onbeing.org/blog/thomas-mertons -prayer-that-anyone-can-pray.

[20]Lewis, *Screwtape Letters*, 49.

[21]Lewis, *Screwtape Letters*, 49.

[22]Stephanie Chen, "Could You be 'Infected' by Friend's Divorce?," CNN, June 10, 2010, http://edition.cnn.com/2010/LIVING/06/10/divorce.contagious.gore/index.html.

[23]Lewis, *Screwtape Letters*, 112.

[24]C. S. Lewis, *Screwtape Proposes a Toast* (Bel Air, CA: Fount, 1993), 120.

[25]Blaise Pascal, *Pensées* 136 (New York: Penguin Books, 1966), 67.

[26]These observations concerning creating pockets of solitude are taken from my book *I Beg to Differ: Navigating Difficult Conversations with Truth and Love* (Downers Grove, IL: InterVarsity Press, 2015), 71-75.

[27]Guy Winch, "How Cellphone Use Can Disconnect Your Relationship," *Psychology Today*, January 15, 2015, www.psychologytoday.com/blog/the-squeaky-wheel/201501 /how-cellphone-use-can-disconnect-your-relationship.

[28]Jamin Goggin and Kyle Strobel, *The Way of the Dragon or the Way of the Lamb* (Nashville: Nelson Books, 2017), 83.

[29]Nancy Sleeth, *Almost Amish: One Woman's Quest for a Slower, Simpler, More Sustainable Life* (Carol Stream, IL: Tyndale House, 2012), 26.

[30]Linda Dillow and Lorraine Pintus, *Intimate Issues: 21 Questions Christian Women Ask About Sex* (Colorado Springs, CO: WaterBrook, 1999), 39.

[31]Dillow and Pintus, *Intimate Issues*, 40.

[32]Lewis, *Screwtape Letters*, 174.

CONCLUSION

[1]Clint Arnold, *Powers of Darkness: Principalities and Powers in Paul's Letters* (Downers Grove, IL: InterVarsity Press, 1992), 163.

ALSO AVAILABLE FROM TIM MUEHLHOFF

Authentic Communication: Christian Speech Engaging Culture, coauthored with Todd V. Lewis

The God Conversation: Using Stories and Illustrations to Explain Your Faith, revised and expanded edition, coauthored with J. P. Moreland

I Beg to Differ: Navigating Difficult Conversations with Truth and Love

Marriage Forecasting: Changing the Climate of Your Relationship One Conversation at a Time

Winsome Persuasion: Christian Influence in a Post-Christian World, coauthored with Richard Langer

Website: www.timmuehlhoff.com

Podcast: The Art of Relationships (http://cmr.biola.edu/podcast/)